The *Gay* Preacher's Wife

The *Gay* Preacher's Wife

*How My Gay Husband Deconstructed
My Life and Reconstructed My Faith*

LYDIA MEREDITH

GALLERY BOOKS   KAREN HUNTER PUBLISHING
New York   London   Toronto   Sydney   New Delhi

G

Gallery Books
An Imprint of Simon & Schuster, Inc.
1230 Avenue of the Americas
New York, NY 10020

Karen Hunter Publishing,
A Division of Suitt-Hunter Enterprises, LLC
598 Broadway, 3rd Floor
New York, NY 10012

First Karen Hunter Publishing/Gallery Books trade paperback edition October 2016

GALLERY BOOKS and colophon are registered trademarks of Simon & Schuster, Inc.

For information about special discounts for bulk purchases, please contact Simon & Schuster Special Sales at 1-866-506-1949 or business@simonandschuster.com.

The Simon & Schuster Speakers Bureau can bring authors to your live event. For more information or to book an event contact the Simon & Schuster Speakers Bureau at 1-866-248-3049 or visit our website at www.simonspeakers.com.

Interior design by Davina Mock-Maniscalco

Manufactured in the United States of America

10   9   8   7   6   5   4   3   2   1

Library of Congress Cataloging-in-Publication Data is available.

ISBN 978-1-4767-8893-7
ISBN 978-1-4767-8894-4 (ebook)

To those crippled by the crime of hate and hypocrisy,
Pick up your bed and walk!

CONTENTS

INTRODUCTION

There's a Leak in This Old Building

1

CHAPTER ONE

Red Flags

15

CHAPTER TWO

Living Single

25

CHAPTER THREE

No Preacher for Me!

41

Contents

CHAPTER FOUR

I Do!

55

CHAPTER FIVE

First Lady Meredith

71

CHAPTER SIX

Picture-Perfect

87

CHAPTER SEVEN

Fix It, Jesus!

97

CHAPTER EIGHT

Sowing the Seeds

117

CHAPTER NINE

Daddy's Girl

133

CHAPTER TEN

Reality Check

145

CHAPTER ELEVEN

The Apple and the Tree

161

Contents

CHAPTER TWELVE

The Diagnosis I

175

CHAPTER THIRTEEN

The Diagnosis II

181

CHAPTER FOURTEEN

The End

191

CHAPTER FIFTEEN

Schooling

201

CHAPTER SIXTEEN

To Forgive . . .

215

EPILOGUE

Mercy and Truth

227

SIGNS

Eight Signs That Your Partner May Be Gay

237

ix

The *Gay* Preacher's Wife

There's a Leak in This Old Building

There's a leak in this old building and my soul . . . has got to move
To another building . . . a building not made by man's hand.
—Lashun Pace

There is a story that made headlines in 2013 about a Memphis pastor who was arrested for sexual battery on a minor. He had been allegedly sexually abusing a sixteen-year-old member of his church for two years. The teen reported the abuse to adults in the church. Instead of turning the pastor in to the authorities, the parishioners only prayed for the pastor.

People were outraged about the church's reaction, just as they were outraged when members of Bishop Eddie Long's New Birth Missionary Baptist Church defended him when he was accused of sexual misconduct with underage boys in his church.

But this denial has been going on in churches for years.

The Catholic Church's offenses represent the most publicized cases of sexual abuse of minors spanning decades. The Vatican not only turned a blind eye to the pedophilia among its ranks, it also covered up the crimes and protected the perpetrators.

This is not a new phenomenon; we just know more about the scandals because of social media and a twenty-four-hour news cycle that demands information. I think it was worse in previous generations, in the era of "children should be seen and not heard." In the times in which I grew up, there was a push to protect so-called leaders whether they were in the church or the White House. We overlooked their flaws for the "greater good."

I grew up in a church where this was the case. Our pastor was a womanizer. He was a notorious womanizer. But no one ever held him accountable. He had several mistresses. I didn't need to hear any rumors; I knew about Pastor Johnson firsthand.

I used to spend a lot of time at the home of Ms. Halston. She was my godmother and she had three children. I would often go to her house to play. Pastor Johnson came over for a visit in the middle of the day while I was there once. It seemed strange to me that the pastor would be there. And while I didn't see them doing anything, I could tell by their nonverbal communication and the way they were moving around each other that something was up. The energy between the two was pretty powerful.

It was said that Ms. Halston was Pastor Johnson's daughter and her mother was Pastor Johnson's mistress. Her children were his grandchildren. (They did look just like him.) Ms. Halston's mother would sit on the back pew with her family on Sunday morning; and everyone whispered about their affair.

I knew Pastor Johnson was a pervert. My sister Tricia (short for Patricia) confessed to me, when we were adults, that Pastor Johnson had tried to have sex with her. She said she told Mother what happened but Mother still insisted that Tricia attend church despite her anguish and emotional duress, repeating the timeless adage, "A family that prays together stays together." In our household, every human being breathing had to get up and go to church together on Sunday morning. Tricia stopped going to church as soon as she moved out of the house! I always wondered why Tricia stopped going to church. I never imagined that what happened to me had also happened to her.

I had my own experience with Pastor Johnson. He used to ask me to teach Sunday school class while he sat and observed. One Sunday, Pastor Johnson put his arm around me and tried to touch me inappropriately. You know a proper touch and an improper touch. I was twelve, middle-school age. I felt very uncomfortable. As the children started leaving, I knew in my gut to follow them out. I didn't want to be alone with him. I didn't even tell my father or my mother, because I was confused and didn't know how to tell. In my family, saying anything about sex or anything with a sexual implication was prohibited! Growing up, my dad worked 24/7, and I didn't have an intimate relationship with my mother—my mother was not a nurturer or easily approachable. With so many siblings, I felt as if I was just one in the pack, with no individual value or identity. I learned, much later in life, as my relationship evolved with my mother, that she suffered the same spousal abuse as Pastor Johnson's wife, as well as childhood abuse and neglect. The fallout of this abuse often took my mother to a distant and incensed emotional space. Most times as a child, I felt I had to take care of myself. Ergo, my response to Pastor Johnson's advances was to avoid being alone in his presence.

I'm sure just about every girl in our church had a Pastor Johnson experience. But no one ever did anything about it. He would be up in that pulpit every Sunday with his big belly and his wavy hair, preaching and sweating. People would be "Amening!" and shouting hysterically. And they would continue to attend and support the church.

His wife, our first lady, was the meanest woman I have ever known. She was meaner than a rattlesnake. I didn't put two and two together, because as a kid, all I knew was that First Lady

Johnson never smiled and never had a kind word for anyone. But as an adult, I understood why she was so mean. I would be angry too if my husband was blatantly cheating on me with just about anyone he desired, and I had to sit in church and pretend as if I didn't know. Her only child, a son, died at an early age and she couldn't have any more children. And here, her husband, the pastor, was having a child with another woman.

In those days, women didn't leave their husbands. They stayed, despite the humiliation. That type of disrespect would have made me angry and mean too.

Pastor Johnson was a respected man in the community. My mother had a picture of him proudly displayed in our living room. (Mother reluctantly removed the picture after Tricia told her, "If you don't remove this picture, I won't be coming home again for another Thanksgiving dinner.")

Pastor Johnson was a savvy businessman. He owned just about every piece of property around the church, which he used to house a school and provide affordable housing. He had a trade school that helped put black men to work after the war. That was in the 1950s and 1960s.

Then, as today, men in powerful positions felt that they could get away with anything. Add being pastor of a church, and that feeling of entitlement goes to a whole new level.

It was the end of September in 2010 and the scandal was heating up. Three young men, who were members of the New Birth Missionary Baptist Church in Atlanta, filed a lawsuit claiming that Bishop Eddie Long had "bought them" with cars, lavish trips, and cash in exchange for sex. It was a scandal that would not only rock the church founded by Long—one of the largest and most prestigious churches in Atlanta—this church hosted the funeral of Coretta Scott King—this scandal, would also put a bright spotlight on the Christian faith.

It was one of a string of recent scandals with preachers, pastors, and church leaders. We had seen Jim Bakker, husband of Tammy Faye and pastor of the Assemblies of God Church and the PTL (Praise the Lord) television ministry go to jail for fraud. We saw Jimmy Swaggart get in front of the world, crying, "I have sinned . . ." when he was busted with prostitutes and removed from the ministry. We had seen Ted Haggard, leader of the National Association of Evangelicals, get caught with a male escort and some crystal meth and have to step down from his church.

But this was different—Eddie Long refused to step down. He had just as many supporters as he had detractors calling for his head. And this case was bigger than Eddie Long. This kind of thing—preachers being disgraced—was becoming so prevalent that people no longer cared as much. Eddie Long became merely a symptom of a greater ill that was infecting our church—hypocrisy. And he was far from alone. By now, I knew this firsthand.

The media reached out to Dennis Meredith, my ex-husband, to respond to the Eddie Long scandal. I understood why they contacted him. His church was the only African-American church in Atlanta to welcome openly gay members. And he had just come out as gay himself. It was a natural fit. But when he called me, and asked me, what I thought about him responding, I said, "No way. Stay out of it!"

I saw that Dennis would have a choice of just two responses: Attempt to explain it and come out in support of Eddie Long—which would have been absurd and disastrous—or condemn Eddie Long. Publicly condemning Eddie Long would have made Dennis a hypocrite of the highest order. While I didn't know him to have sexual relations with minors, Dennis was (a middle-aged pastor) living with a boyfriend who was twenty-something years old when they got together—the affair started while Dennis was still married to me. There would be countless scandals to uncover in Dennis's life if the media wanted to start digging. I thought it was best that he stay out of the mess, and I thought he should definitely not throw a single stone at Eddie Long. I didn't think anyone should be out there throwing stones, because none of us is without fault. But Dennis responded anyway.

And the hypocrisy grew.

Bernice King, a daughter of Martin Luther King Jr., who was a member of Eddie Long's New Birth Missionary Baptist Church, left his congregation. I laughed at that one. In 2004,

Bernice King and Eddie Long led a march near Freedom Parkway, of all places, which leads to the Martin Luther King Jr. National Historic Site, an emblem of freedom and justice. The march was against gay marriage.

In the Atlanta gay community, this was a travesty because homosexual rumors had long been swirling about Long. So this march was simply disingenuous and political. The march against gay marriage got a lot of media attention. However, there was also an Atlanta gay magazine that threatened to "out" Long if he didn't stop his hypocritical, bigoted behavior. When I saw Long and Bernice King on television, holding those torches and speaking out against the ills of homosexuality, I thought to myself, *We're in trouble here.*

We weren't in trouble because Long or King might both be gay and were leading a march against gays. The trouble was deeper than that: The focus of the church changed from inspiring, healing, empowering, saving, and restoring broken lives and communities to the "politics of religion"—a serious disconnect from the real purpose and mission of Jesus Christ.

Fast-forward and the Eddie Long scandal hits, and he settles out of court with those young boys, and Bernice King leaves his church and all of a sudden changes her stance on gays and gay marriage. But the real issues still haven't been addressed.

What's really going wrong within the church?

On any given Sunday and most early mornings and late

nights, you can turn on your television and see preachers with congregations so big that they have to hold services in a football stadium or a basketball arena. They are preaching prosperity and other things that may be good, but you have to ask yourself, *Where's God in all of this?* And while it's great that they have so many attending their churches and events, are they really feeding their flocks? This question rephrased in lay vernacular: Are churches today in the business of helping people, families, and society?

I turn on the television and see preachers and preachers' wives and families on reality TV shows. They aren't talking about how their ministries are improving lives and the community. They are talking about themselves. We're looking at their quirks, their possessions, their relationships—we're getting charged up and entertained because of the conflict and tension in their relationships. It's like a soap opera.

Some of these pastors have the status of rock stars and celebrities. They drive Bentleys and Rolls-Royces and own private jets. They live in 15,000-square-foot mansions and have bodyguards. The church and preaching today is business, serious business—but not necessarily God's business—as it markets hate, oppression, political agenda, narcissism, and materialism. The church has become a predator, crippling society and intensifying its perversion.

The church used to be about reaching the masses with the kinds of things that promote love, healing, unity, and bring positive change to families and communities. The majority of churches today are not a part of the conversation or solution: to reduce blight and crime in our communities; to challenge systems that incarcerate and murder young boys of color; to break the cycle of poverty (reducing school dropouts and teenage pregnancy and multiple unwed births [biological fathers unknown]); to remove drugs and drug lords from our street corners, which are literally destroying the institution of families, neighborhoods, and communities; to hold schools accountable to educate our children (our sons and daughters will not reach third grade unable to read) and will be formidable scholars in America and globally. In summary, sermon content and church programming are far removed from healing and transforming broken and dysfunctional families and depraved conditions in our communities.

When I was growing up, we had Father Divine and Reverend Ike. But they weren't the norm. And they got a lot of criticism from pastors around the country that looked at them as undermining the work of God. Today, Father Divine and Reverend Ike would be the norm. Ministers have become popular and wealthy, by promoting themes of instant personal wealth or instant physical health or hate, through sensationalism, misrepresentations, and superstition. This has become the norm.

To the contrary, the church exists to "be rich" in good deeds, which mitigate the ills of our society and to shine light on God and point humankind to God, its Founder.

We're a far cry from that church described in the Book of Acts more than two thousand years ago. Despite being tortured, mass murdered, and losing their lives, the first-century church was hallmarked by loving, serving, and meeting the needs of others. This church preached and embraced the practice of love and acceptance. This church lived out the values it professed. This church honored the message and legacy of Jesus Christ.

For me, this is all very personal and hit very close to home.

I was one of those preachers' wives who sat in the pew many a Sunday morning while my "real" life was a fraud. I discovered several years into my marriage that my husband was cheating on me—with men—numerous men. (And women too, I later found out). But I stayed. I stayed through the broken promises and the humiliation because I believed and hoped that things would get better. I watched my husband stand in that pulpit on Sunday morning, preaching one message and living out yet another. I needed answers.

The first place I turned to for answers was God. I prayed. I wept. I prayed. I wept. I prayed and I wept. God woke me at 3 a.m. in the morning, I sat straight up in the middle of my bed, before the break of dawn. I said out loud to myself, "I'm going back to school." So, I went back to school to earn a master's degree in religion with an emphasis on Christian education to get some answers. What did Jesus really say about homosexuality? What was Jesus' message about gays? I wanted to be an authority on the subject that had ripped my family apart. I prayed my entire young life for God to send me a husband—God always answers my prayers—why did I end up marrying a gay man? My middle son is gay and HIV positive: how in the world did this happen—three sons, same incubator, same environment, conceived by the same parents, yet two sons are heterosexual and one son is homosexual—is this biological, genetic, what? My traditional brand of Christianity could not answer these questions—I needed God to help me understand, to reconcile my faith tradition with the facts of my life, to heal my broken heart.

Here's what I found: Jesus never mentions homosexuality. If Jesus, infinitely wise, the founder of our faith, thought it was so important—surely Jesus would have broached the subject "head on." Jesus had prime opportunity to broach the subject—when he reflected upon the sin of Sodom (Luke 10:12)—but he didn't—he lifted from this story one point—be hospitable and kind to strangers. Surely if Jesus felt same-sex love was abhorrent—he would have stated this explicitly in the text—knowing that 2,000 years later, this subject would create a great political and religious debate and divide—but he didn't.

Jesus' entire ministry was hallmarked by "inclusion" of society's rejects. And Jesus' ministry and teachings actually show more tolerance and love for people who are labeled different—than the church and preachers currently preach—from the Catholics (before Pope Francis) to the evangelical movement.

What I did find was this: The church needs a new kind of ministry—one steeped in the tradition of the ministry "started" by Jesus—free of bias, discrimination, hate, or prejudice; and marked by loving God and loving others—the key to social transformation.

"Faith hate and hypocrisy" is the paradox that has arrested my life's attention. Edgar G. Hawkins said, "The church is implicated in the sickness of our society, because it failed to protect its own values." Lifted from politically and economically charged interpretations of the biblical texts are the notions that God condemns homosexuals to hell; God condemns people of color to a life of slavery/servitude; and God condemns women to certain life roles and conditions. Oppression and discrimination that thrives in society are fueled and justified by these debated, unsubstantiated notions that are not upheld by the teachings of Jesus and the life practice of Jesus. Jesus as the perfect revelation of God is truth. Ergo, the church must begin to live and preach the truth: to lay aside foolishness—thought and practice that impedes peace, harmony and right living—and secure and uphold thought and practice that saves and transforms lives and communities.

So I'm going to share my story, my truth, in hopes that it inspires people (who are oppressed and made ill by faith hate and hypocrisy) to pick up your sick beds and walk—walk in truth. I hope that my story will inspire love, expressed best through forgiveness. I pray it will move society to a consciousness of accountability, responsibility, and an acceptance and tolerance of diversity (race, sexuality, ethnicity, gender, ability, personality), a diversity intentionally created by God. And most important, I hope that my story will lead us all to a deeper understanding and loving relationship with God and God's greatest creation—humankind.

CHAPTER ONE

Red Flags

In 1978, we were living in Birmingham, Alabama. Dennis was the youth minister at Sardis Baptist Church. He had just quit his day job to go back to school full-time to get his degree.

I was supporting the family financially, working at U.S. Steel Corporation–Fairfield Works, as an engineer making a great salary with greater benefits. I worked long hours—sometimes ten-hour days. But I enjoyed my work and I loved coming home to our four-bedroom, two-bath house, home to my perfect family.

In 1979, our first son, Taylor was born; and fifteen months later, Micah was born. Each son had his own room, but they were so close that it wouldn't be unusual to wake up and find Taylor, the oldest, sleeping in his little brother Micah's crib.

If I worked late, Dennis would make sure dinner was cooked. Every night we would eat together as a family. After dinner most evenings, Dennis would head off to the church for meetings, choir rehearsal, to prepare for Sunday, or to study or do homework. When he got home, if I was still awake, we would make love. That was most nights and that was our life. I loved every minute of it.

The call came around one in the morning, startling me out of my sleep. I never waited up for Dennis, but he hadn't come home yet, which was unusual this time of night. I was instantly alarmed.

"Hello," I said.

The voice on the other end was gruff.

"Your husband has been arrested for assaulting a police officer," said the voice on the other end, whose owner identified himself as a police officer.

I was petrified and baffled. Last I knew, Dennis was at a church function. How could that end up with him having a confrontation with a police officer? And being arrested?

It had to be a prank call. We were talking about Dennis Meredith, a youth pastor, a devoted husband and father, living in a nice house in a middle-class neighborhood. He was a pillar of the community. Arrested? This just didn't add up.

I called my neighbor whose husband worked for the police department and told her about the phone call. I asked if her husband would check it out for me. He confirmed that Dennis had indeed been arrested.

Now what? I had two babies under the age of three, and somebody was telling me to come downtown to get my husband out of jail. I asked my neighbor next door to come and watch the boys, who were asleep. I wasn't going to downtown Birmingham in the middle of the night by myself. I then called Dr. Crowley, one of Dennis's religion professors at Samford University.

Dennis had actually already called Dr. Crowley to come and bail him out. In fact, Dennis never did call me. He didn't want me to know he had been arrested. The police department called me. Dr. Crowley and I bailed Dennis out. On the ride to the jailhouse, I was overwhelmed by a series of emotions. I was stunned and in shock. I think I suppressed the pain. Suppression was my natural coping mechanism—always had been. Denial! Suppression! Or complete avoidance!

I felt comatose, as if this was happening to someone else and I was watching it. When I entered the police station, I found my husband right there out front in handcuffs as one white officer talked with another about his release. His head was hanging down slightly. I don't think he wanted to look at me. I don't know if he could.

I learned from the officer who'd booked him that Dennis hadn't been arrested for assaulting a police officer. What he'd been arrested for was soliciting an undercover police officer—a *male* undercover officer. What did that mean, exactly? I wasn't trying to wrap my mind around what it meant at this time. Denial! Suppression! Avoidance!

Dennis was in an adult theater. It was the kind of theater that was known for a certain kind of sexual activity. There was an undercover police officer in the theater. The undercover police officer approached Dennis, saying, "What do you want to do?" Dennis replied, "I want to get my dick sucked." The police officer then turned his back to Dennis, and pulled out his badge. Then, he turned around and said, "You're under arrest for soliciting a police officer."

I had no words. They released him on his own recognizance. And Dr. Crowley drove us home. There was no talking on that drive. Not a word. I had no words for Dennis, and I'm sure he didn't want to talk about it, either. When Dr. Crowley pulled up to the house, I jumped out of the car and went inside, leaving Dennis with Dr. Crowley. I was angry, but I was something else that I couldn't identify at the same time.

Dr. Crowley came in, and he and Dennis sat at our dining room table, and Dennis started to cry.

"I'm sorry," he sobbed. "I'm so sorry."

I went to bed, not saying a word to either Dennis or Dr. Crowley.

The next day, Dennis tried to act as if it wasn't a big deal. He tried to brush it off as nothing. The words *gay* and *homosexual* never came up. He made it seem as if he'd just been looking for a release, and I didn't want to press him. I wasn't ready to confront the truth that was staring me right in the face. I didn't even make the gay connection that Dennis had asked a *man* to suck his dick. I was fixated on him asking anyone to perform a sex act on him. I was always there for him in that way. Why did he need to have anyone else, but me?

I was also concerned about the scandal of him—a noted pastor—getting arrested. Thank goodness we were able to keep that a secret. Our neighbor and her husband were no longer members of the church, but they didn't tell anyone. At least, it never got out. Dennis ended up getting a slap on the wrist and the charges dropped.

It would be impossible to keep that arrest a secret today. But this was the early 1980s. There was no TMZ, no social media, no twenty-four-hour news cycle.

Dennis's arrest was the first sign that I should have paid attention to. It was a big, flashing, hot-pink neon sign, and my response to it was to simply decide to shut my eyes and pretend the obvious wasn't there.

Dennis apologized profusely. He called me at work and asked me to meet him in the stairwell during my break. It had been a few days, and we hadn't touched or talked since the incident. He held me tight as if his life depended on it.

"I'm so sorry," he kept saying.

"Do you promise this will never happen again?" I asked.

"I promise," he said.

It was the first of many promises he'd break over the years.

I can now admit to being naïve regarding the whole homosexuality thing. It just wasn't something people talked about back then—especially not in the black community. The black community still has trouble talking about it today.

I knew gay people. One of my best friends at Vanderbilt University, where I had attended college, was gay. My best friends on campus were two guys—Cecil and Jackie. Jackie was openly gay and was ostracized, so I took him under my wing. I was raised in a family that fought for the underdog, so that was my nature. With both of my parents being outcasts (by class) and homeless at points in their lives, it was nothing for them to take in someone from the streets, if just for a hot meal. So when I saw how some people on campus were treating Jackie, making fun of him and acting as if he had the plague, I made sure to make him my friend.

I loved hanging out with him—especially since there was no pressure or possibility that he would hit on me. Cecil was in a committed relationship with a girl he loved, so our relationship was also perfect. (To this day, Cecil and Sarah, the woman who would become his wife, are still my friends.)

As far as Jackie being gay, he was flamboyantly gay. That was something I had seen and understood—men who were feminine and colorful and obviously gay. I didn't understand that a man like Dennis, a six-foot-four, strong, muscular, manly man, could be gay. Openly, not hiding, girly gay—I got that. Dennis gay?! I couldn't see it—especially since he was always after me to have sex with him. He seemed not to be able to get enough of me sexually.

Dennis was a preacher. He was a man of God. I knew that he loved his family. He was a great father. He was a good husband. He was a fantastic lover. How could he be gay? My life with him was perfect. And I wasn't willing to rock the boat of my "perfect" life. Not over a blow job in a movie theater that hadn't actually taken place.

Gay? No way!

Dennis was the best sexual partner in the world. In *my* world! He knew my body. He knew exactly what to do. I had an orgasm every single time. He brought creativity to our love life. There was no telling what we were going to do next sexually. I looked forward to making love to my husband, and we did so quite frequently.

He was so spontaneous. One day I came home from work and he said, "Let's go!" He didn't tell me where we were going, but the whole drive was sensual, with him touching me and me touching him in our hot spots all the way. Then finally we arrived. It was a place with private baths, Jacuzzis, and steam rooms. We checked in and got fresh towels and linens. We entered our room and it was amazing. Every inch of my body was aroused and so was his. We undressed each other and the adventure began. We spent the whole afternoon there.

Afterward, he took me to a romantic dinner. He literally wined and dined me. Dennis brought balance to the relationship. I was the one who worked all the time, and Dennis brought fun and energy. Most of the fun we had—from spousal bliss to family joy—was because of Dennis.

I was madly and completely in love with this man. *Gay?* Absolutely not!

There were some other signs that should have set off alarms for me. But Dennis always had a story or an excuse that seemed to make sense, and I believed him. I wanted to believe him. He gave me crabs a short time after we got married, before we had kids. I had no idea what it was; I just knew I had a horrible itch. I showed it to Dennis and he looked at it and was real nonchalant. "Oh, that's just crabs," he said. He bought some medication from the drugstore and treated me and it went away.

He told me he had them too but hadn't thought I would get them also. When I questioned him about it, he said he must have gotten them from a toilet seat. Dennis was notorious for having a very regular digestion system. When he ate, he would always have to go to the bathroom shortly thereafter. If we went out to dinner, he would definitely have to use the restroom. So it made sense to me that he had caught crabs from a toilet seat. And I had no reason to question him.

I had to get hit over the head before I would actually accept that (1) my husband was gay/bisexual; (2) my husband was constantly cheating on me; and (3) my marriage was a lie.

That day did come—but not before a lot of years of happiness and delusion, pain and joy, and burying my head in the sand. Looking back, it's easy for me to beat up on myself. But today I understand that I'm not unusual. There are women and men throughout this world in relationships with people who are not what they appear to be. And they stay even when they see the signs, because for many of us, we live with the misconception that it's easier to be in a relationship and live a lie; than to confront the truth and be alone. Sometimes people stay because of their lack of self-worth. When Dennis and I went to counseling to save our marriage, we discovered that we suffered with low self-esteem because of our dysfunctional families of origin. And that our lack of self-love was the force behind so many unhealthy and harmful decisions. I made the choice to stay.

For me, I just really loved this man. I wanted to be with him until the day I died. I didn't want our marriage to ever end. And I was willing to do anything to see that it didn't end. I loved my family and I loved my life.

But eventually, I had to learn to love myself more.

CHAPTER TWO

Living Single

S ex was taboo growing up. Nobody talked about it—not my mother, not my father, not my siblings. I was raised in a very strict, churchgoing family—one of ten children. People were having sex, for sure. But no one talked about it.

In fact, it was as if *sex* was a dirty word in my world. I grew up in the 1950s and 1960s, the so-called sexual revolution hit the United States, according to most historians, between the late 1940s and 1960s. By the time I was headed to college, the fall of 1970, the feminist movement was in full swing. Women were burning their bras and demanding equality. In the 1970s, when I was becoming an adult, birth control, or "the pill," was becoming popular. Abortion was legalized following the landmark decision in *Roe v. Wade*. And there was a book that was taking the nation by storm: *The Joy of Sex* was published in 1972, spending eleven weeks on the *New York Times* bestseller list.

But all of that was lost on me. In my world in the South, with my strict Christian upbringing, bra burning, birth control, and abortions weren't on my radar. Women's rights?! That freedom hadn't made its way to the church community. I never had *that* talk—not with my parents, not with my sisters. Not with anyone. I just had to figure things out when the time came.

I didn't even know how a woman got pregnant until I got to college. I know that sounds crazy, but it's the truth. All I knew was that if you got pregnant, you couldn't go back home. I knew you got pregnant messing around with boys, so I just avoided them altogether. I didn't get my period until I was sixteen. I was a late bloomer.

I didn't have a clue about sex, let alone homosexuality. When I became sexually active, I didn't really enjoy it much—not until I met Dennis. He awakened in me things I never knew existed. I loved how he made me feel. Beyond that, I was clueless.

I earned a full academic scholarship to attend Vanderbilt University in Nashville. My first year at Vanderbilt was a real culture shock. I was totally unprepared for what I was to experience. I walked in to the Branscomb Quadrangle, where the entire freshman female class was housed. No boys were allowed to visit, except for the lobby. And there was a strict curfew—even on weekends. Despite this strictness, we still had freshman girls dropping out first semester because they got pregnant—some had illegal abortions. I was shocked. I got to see a lot of things personally because of my roommate.

There were about thirty blacks on the entire campus at Vanderbilt in 1970. Coming from my high school, I was used to being one of a handful of blacks. And we all pretty much hung out together. My roommate was from New Jersey. She talked so fast I could barely understand a word she said. Her SAT scores were much higher than mine, and her parents were high society—her dad was an engineer and she was following in his footsteps, majoring in engineering. She was very pretty and popular. She had her pick of the few black guys on campus.

She was on birth control pills, and she slipped her boyfriend into our room for sex every day. I was shocked and appalled. We couldn't have been more different. She was having sex all the time. And I had never had sex.

I did have a boyfriend in high school, Joey. He played basketball and taught me how to play, and he was very good-looking. We made it to second base (sensual kissing), but that was it. I really liked Joey. But my mother thought he was beneath me because he came from a poor family. That seemed strange to me because we were poor too. But Mother was always talking to us about "marrying up," and finding people who came from educated and well-to-do families for mates. Joey ended up going into the army. He used to write me all the time. In one of his letters he told me he was horny. I had no idea what that meant, and I showed it to my sister Cookie. She told me it meant he wanted to have sex with me. I sent him back this scathing letter saying, "How dare you say such a thing to me?!"

I just didn't get it. My first week at Vanderbilt I got a letter from Joey. I was so excited until I read it. He broke up with me. He said he was breaking up with me because I didn't really love him. He said if I loved him, I would want to be with him in that way. I was so hurt. I poured myself into my studies.

I wasn't interested in dating anyone. There were a few guys on campus who wanted to take me out, and finally, toward the end of the first semester, I decided to go out with Jeff. He was on the basketball team and very handsome. I was the only black cheerleader at the school, and he was the only black basketball player on the team at the time. So we had something in common.

We went out a few times after the game. One time, he escorted me back to my dorm.

"I couldn't keep my eyes off of you during the game," he said, talking of me cheerleading on the sidelines. "I'm sure I missed a few plays."

I blushed. He held my hand and asked me to go with him to his dorm room.

"I'm telling you right now, I don't have sex with boys," I told him, snatching my hand away.

He said, "Really? Well, who *do* you have sex with?"

I laughed with him. And that warmed me up. He picked my hand back up and we headed toward his room.

"Okay, I'm going to your room just to see what it looks like," I told him. "I'm not going to have sex."

I stuck to my guns that time, but I really started to like Jeff, and in the back of my mind was a swirl of emotions. I was in college. I was a grown woman. I was away from home. Maybe it was time I learned what all the fuss was about. My roommate made it seem as if she couldn't live without sex. Was it that good? Then there was Joey. His letter. I'd lost Joey because I wouldn't have sex with him. After one game, and our usual walk back to the dorm, I not only went up to check out Jeff's room, but I finally had sex.

When it was over, all I could think was, *That was it?* And I was ashamed over having done it.

I left his room thinking I could have waited even longer to do that. I also thought that sex was just for men, because I received no gratification. But I didn't want to lose another boyfriend, and it appeared to be just what women did. So I became Jeff's girlfriend. Of course, after doing it with him, I just knew Jeff was the one. We would now have to get married. I was raised with this strict religious background, and that was what was supposed to happen. I was so stupid. I wish someone had told me something.

He was my first love, and I was pretty happy. But coming into our sophomore year, Jeff announced that he was dating someone else, a freshman at Tennessee State University. After he got what he wanted, he seemed to lose interest in me. I was heartbroken and wanted to leave school. I called home and told my mother I wanted to transfer to the University of Georgia or someplace closer to home. My mother, Annie Mae, said, "You are staying." But she didn't speak with her usual, detached, un-sympathetic tone. There was more compassion.

"Always keep you at least two or three boyfriends. Don't get serious with any of them. And have fun! You got a scholarship to get your education. Get your degree and have fun. Don't get serious with anybody."

I took my mother's advice. I enjoyed the rest of my time at Vanderbilt hanging out with my friends Cecil and Jackie. I also reconnected with my best friends from high school, Trish, who went to Spelman College, and Linda, who went to Fisk University, right across the tracks from Vanderbilt. Trish was dating a pro-football hopeful, and Linda had made up her mind to marry a doctor from Meharry Medical College (which she did).

I was dating *two* pre-med students—one from Fisk and one from Vanderbilt.

After Jeff dumped me, I also got dropped from the cheer-leading squad the next year. The first year, I'd made the team based on scores. They changed the rules the following year to a voting system. I tried out and had perfect scores again, but I wasn't voted on. There were only thirty or so blacks in the entire school and I didn't have enough votes. Besides the fact, I didn't look white (or pass for white)—I was thin and dark-skinned with nappy hair.

I didn't pout or miss it. I decided it was an opportunity to do something different. I became very Afro-centric. I changed my hairstyle, sometimes wearing an Afro and sometimes wearing cornrows. I joined the campus African-American Association, of which Cecil was the president. I started a gospel choir on campus, which ended up winning a school-wide singing contest.

What started off as a horrible experience that made me want to leave ended up being the catalyst for one of the best times of my life. I kept a couple of boyfriends (as my mother suggested), and I was more focused on my outside activities, my friends, and excelling in my studies. I joined the only black sorority on campus, Alpha Kappa Alpha, and I made the dean's list. I even had a couple of part-time jobs. I graduated from Vanderbilt with a BS in engineering and a master's in business (on a full scholarship). And I had career offers all over the country.

I wanted to stay in the South. So I accepted a position with U.S. Steel Corporation—Fairfield Works in Birmingham.

This was the summer of 1975. I was the first black in the management-training program at U.S. Steel. I was even featured in the local newspaper—Affirmative Action at its best! It was a travesty to see that all the blacks worked in the mills and all the management was white. Women were either secretaries or janitors. I was really breaking new ground.

My first day at work, I was so excited. I walked into a three-story office building and continued into the offices of the industrial engineering department. There were two secretaries (both white) and eleven white men.

I walked in the door, all ninety pounds of me, put on my best smile, and said, "Good morning!" to everyone. My voice filled the large room without a microphone—cheerleading taught me voice projection. A few people looked up from whatever they were doing to look at me. But most didn't even acknowledge my presence. And no one said good morning back.

My direct supervisor was a huge man; however, everyone had big stomachs that hung over their belts. My supervisor had to have weighed more than two hundred and fifty pounds—mostly grit and muscle. He had gray hair and wore dark-rimmed glasses. He was very intimidating! The whole time he was training me to program the computers used to test steel samples for the correct chemical composition/steel recipes, all he talked about was Bull Connor, the head of the police and fire departments of Birmingham. During the civil rights movement, Connor ordered the attack on peaceful black demonstrators by vicious dogs, firehoses, and club-happy police officers.

"Bull Connor was a great man," my supervisor would say nonchalantly while showing me some code to enter into the computer. "He really knew how to run a city. That Bull Connor was something else."

Heck, this man looked like Bull Connor or one of those racist characters from a civil rights movie. He was the most racist man I had ever met.

Every day he would have his coffee, his cigarette, and his Bull Connor praise hour.

I wanted to quit. It was torture working under these conditions, but I remembered what my mother always used to say to me: "Don't treat them the way they treat you. Kill them with kindness."

What I learned from my parents about hospitality and service, forgiveness and being a Christian, helped me cope in this hostile environment.

I had worked for white folks all my life, since I was ten: washing, ironing, babysitting, as a cashier, as a receptionist in a laboratory, as a secretary. No job was too big or too small. No job was too demeaning or too challenging. I watched my parents work this system of institutionalized racism to resist dependence on welfare, own property, send all of us to college on meager earnings, and push us all to make good grades in school so that we could earn scholarships. My parents taught us how to survive!

So I blocked out the rude comments by Mr. Racist and kept saying good morning every day to the entire office, whether it was returned or not. I don't remember when it happened, but eventually people started saying good morning back. Even "Bull Connor, Jr." warmed up to me, and we ended up becoming friends. He even came to my wedding years later.

I learned so much working at the steel plant. It was tough work. On days I had to be in the plant, wearing blue jeans, a hard hat, a fire jacket, goggles, and metatarsal boots with steel toes. The plant was primitive. Today it would be in violation of every kind of code imaginable. There was a thick haze of black residue in the air over the plant. The pollution was that visible. Outside of the steelmaking process control computers, office equipment and practice were so archaic. They used adding machines and manually created and kept their books, ledgers, and spreadsheets.

I learned so much, though. I learned so fast and so well that I moved up the ladder to upper management very quickly. The computer and management skills I learned also came in handy for my family. Thanks to what I learned there, I was able to write a payroll computer program/software for my sister Cookie's medical services outsourcing business, Med-Tech. I also installed the computers and programs/software for another sister (Faye) to manage her string of beauty salons in Florida, called All Dolled Up.

When I arrived in Birmingham, I had saved enough money from summer jobs to pay the deposit and first month's rent on a nice apartment in Bessemer, Alabama. My brother Lloyd (a mechanical genius and Vietnam veteran) came to visit me to help me pick out a used (sorry, pre-owned) car to drive to and from work.

Lloyd picked out a 1972 Chevelle Malibu that I named Sadie. Sadie was three years old. Sadie ran like a scolded dog, never broke down, and always cranked up, even on cold mornings. I was determined to keep Sadie until she couldn't run anymore, and that's exactly what happened. She started out with a vinyl top; it came loose and I would be speeding down the highway with the vinyl top flying in the wind. I finally got it fixed. I didn't care too much about what people said about me. I didn't have a fancy car or a fancy apartment (I had no furniture), and I didn't wear fancy clothes.

I was focused on my career and my two boyfriends who lived out of town. My brother Lloyd, a man of few words, told me when he left town after helping me get Sadie, "Lydia, find you a church to join, pay your tithes, and God will bless you."

I did what Lloyd said.

While at Vanderbilt, one of my classmates and sorors, whose hair always looked so nice, lived in Birmingham. I called and asked her to introduce me to her hairdresser. She did. Mrs. Laura did hair out of the basement of her house. She had this little dog that barked at you the whole time until you reached the entrance of her basement salon. Mrs. Laura ignored how annoyed her customers were, because she really loved this dog. But you put up with it, because Mrs. Laura could do some hair. She knew how to straighten out every—and I mean every—kink on your head. For me, this was torture, because I had a head full of kinks.

We got to talking one day, and I was telling Mrs. Laura how my brother told me I needed to find a church home. She invited me to hers that Sunday, and I went. Sardis Baptist was in a real old, dark building. I got there late and sat in the back. I didn't get to see much of the service, and I didn't really like the setting. It was old and moldy.

After service, Mrs. Laura sought me out. She was so happy to see me. She told me that the church was in the process of moving to another location. The next time I went, the church had moved to the Graymount Avenue location. They had bought this beautiful church that was once an all-white church. The whole area had once been white, but white flight had changed the demographics quickly. I was on time this time, and when I went in, I thought, *Wow!*

I wasn't accustomed to African Americans having a church so beautiful. The church I grew up in might as well have been a barn. There were four or five families that made up the whole church. It had about ten pews total. But the new church home for Sardis was like a cathedral. I said to myself, *Okay, they are a progressive group. They're trying to keep moving up. I can settle in here.*

I started going to Sardis Baptist Church regularly. Reverend Samuel Banks was the pastor. One Sunday, he did a whole sermon on paying your tithes. I didn't really know what tithing was because that wasn't something preached in my church. When I found out it was 10 percent of my *gross* pay, I said no way. I reasoned I had nothing, as well as siblings still at home struggling: why should I give the church 10 percent of my gross pay, or even my net pay? I set up a meeting with the pastor to argue my position and let him know that this was something I couldn't do.

When I went in to talk to Pastor Banks, he simply opened the Bible to the third chapter of Malachi and read it. After this exchange, I started paying my tithes. And the blessings followed, as the Lord and my brother Lloyd said they would. After only working two and a half years, I was able to purchase my very own home. I was twenty-five years old. My boss had to write a letter to my lender to support my loan application because to own property was unprecedented for a single woman, let alone a single *black* woman living in the South during this time.

My friends warned me that I had better not make such a huge investment with my salary. Suppose I got fired, they said.

I told my friends that God promised to meet all my needs if I surrendered to the divine teaching on stewardship and that I was going to bank on that promise.

This home was the first of many homes I would buy and sell over the years. I never missed paying my tithes since I made the commitment more than forty years ago. I worked hard Monday through Friday. I partied every weekend with my girlfriends and went to church every Sunday at Sardis. I took tennis classes and played tennis every day after work when the weather permitted. I took swimming lessons from the American Red Cross, and went from beginning swimmer to senior lifeguard. I took ballet classes, volunteered at the juvenile court for first-time offenders, volunteered at the church teaching teens in Sunday school, sang in the choir, and attended weekly Bible classes. I made sure my days were full so that when I got home I was totally exhausted and slept like a baby.

But I was still lonely. While I dated several men, I had no serious prospect on the horizon. And I wanted a companion with whom to share the rest of my life.

A dear friend of mine, who happened to be a Catholic priest, asked me, "Lydia, what are you going to do with this big ol' house?" I told him, with a hearty, full laugh, "I'm going to get married and put some children in it."

It was the mid-1970s and I was twenty-five years old. I was making moves, moves that most women were not making: I owned my own home and was working my way up the corporate ladder.

But I was unsuccessful in most people's eyes in one area—my personal life. My mother was worried that I would end up an old maid. I watched two of my younger sisters get married, and I still wasn't close to heading down the aisle to the altar.

I had been dating Will and Bill since college. Both were in medical school, out of state, so I also dated a few guys in Birmingham. I liked Will more than the others and we had been going out for more than six years. So, I thought it was time we started talking about marriage. I brought up the subject and started getting a little pushy.

A few days after returning from a visit with him in Florida, I got a letter from him. It was another one of those Dear John letters. I guess men felt more comfortable writing me to break up than telling me to my face. He wrote to tell me that not only was he not ready for marriage, but he was not interested in staying in a relationship with me.

I was hurt because, I thought, *If not Will, then who?* Am I destined to be single the rest of my life? I knew we were not very compatible because Will was so selfish—he made a federal case out of sharing a cup of ice cream. I really didn't feel as though he was my soul mate. And I wasn't really missing out on anything not being with him (especially in the bedroom).

As I do, whenever I am deeply sad and confused, I cried out to God. I was driving and praying, in route to Bible study. "God, I guess I'm going to be by myself for the rest of my life."

It seemed, that just for a moment, time stood still, and God's voice emerged in my broken spirit, saying, "Dennis Meredith will be your husband." I responded quietly, "What will I have to do?" The voice simply said, "Nothing." When I arrived at Bible study, Dennis was the first person I saw; our eyes met for the first time. I had known him from church, he was the youth pastor, but I absolutely had no physical attraction for this man, or any other kind of attraction. I didn't want to date a preacher, let alone be married to a preacher. But after the epiphany, I could not take my eyes or my mind off this man, Dennis Meredith.

CHAPTER THREE

No Preacher for Me!

I was sitting in my regular seat in the choir stand at Sardis Baptist Church in Alabama one Sunday morning. The new youth pastor, who'd arrived from Toledo, Ohio, was finally getting a chance to preach the main service. I remember him sitting in that pulpit, looking as if he was sitting on a throne. His head was held high, his face serious and intense. He looked as if that pulpit was made just for him.

The music was really good this particular Sunday, and

during a certain hymn, I could hear his voice clearly, even from the pulpit. He was really getting into it.

When he stood to preach, the show began. Our regular minister was a bit reserved. He did not stray from the biblical text, and he spoke in forceful but measured tones. But this pastor started off shouting. During some point during his sermon, he walked out of the pulpit and was marching up and down the aisles of the church. He even stood in an empty seat in a pew at one point.

I thought, *This man must be out of his mind. What is he doing?*

I was not into it at all. And I wasn't alone. I could see quite a few other members shaking their heads in disgust. I had never seen anything like it. I was in shock.

This was the first time I noticed Dennis Meredith. This first impression left a lot to be desired.

I learned that he came from a charismatic-Baptist background. Charismatic worship is known to be a bit more enthusiastic in their praise—speaking in tongues, etc. Dennis had grown up in Toledo in one of those shouting churches with a strong music tradition, with drums and tambourines. Their choir was known all over the country, and they had an awesome band. Singing, drums, shouting and the Holy Ghost were staples in Dennis's church experience. And he brought that spirit with him to Sardis.

While many people didn't quite understand him, and quite

a few didn't care for him at all, he certainly stood out. And the children and youth loved him.

Dennis was not just the youth pastor; he also taught Sunday school. He grew that youth ministry from about twenty children, when he took it over, to more than one hundred in less than two years. Sardis Baptist Church had never seen anybody with that type of energy, passion, and impact.

Dennis never tried to talk to me, and I didn't care. I wasn't paying much attention to him, either. He was dating a young lady from the church and I was dating someone too. Dennis simply wasn't my type. He was always dressed to kill, but he clearly wasn't high society. He wasn't attractive to me.

The men I was interested in were educated—medical school students, lawyers and law school students, accountants. When I finished school, I imagined myself married to a professional man with a solid family background. That's what my mother drilled into us, to marry "up." I wanted someone who would bring wealth to the relationship—a doctor, lawyer, or Indian chief (you know, as that childhood song goes). My husband had to be rich or on his way. I figured I could convert him to Christianity if he wasn't in church. I never looked for or expected to find a mate in church.

I had financial goals and a vision for a certain kind of lifestyle. I needed someone who was driven and accomplished. And Dennis didn't seem to fit into that category.

So when Mrs. Laura suggested that I date Dennis, my answer was an emphatic "No way, he's a religious fanatic." Every mother at church was trying to hook him up with her daughter.

He was especially taken with Ellen, a small, thin girl with impeccable manners and poise. Though I was small and thin as well, I was unlike Ellen in every other way. I worked at a steel mill, and how I behaved was determined by my own volition— loud, friendly, and funny.

I was the largest contributor to the church and dressed the worst and drove the worst-looking car. I did my Christian duty, as I had been taught all my life, and that meant going to church, being generous, and helping people. I learned this from my parents. We didn't have much money, so our tithing was always in the form of service, and it was never limited. My parents served whoever was in need, and that's how all of us were raised. But all that other stuff about being appropriate, prim, and proper escaped me. I was the least likely candidate to be married to a preacher.

After breaking up with Will, being broken in spirit, crying out to God in despair, and God "announcing" to me that Dennis Meredith would be my husband—all "my" plans became immaterial—something miraculous happened in that moment which changed my disposition for Dennis. And I know Dennis's disposition toward me changed too, because after Bible study, Dennis walked me to my car and said he thought I was a nice person and wanted to get to know me better. So I invited him to dinner.

I asked Pastor Banks to tell me what Dennis liked to eat, so that I could impress him with his favorite home-cooked meal. Little did I know that the pastor did not want me dating Dennis and thought it was not a good idea. He told me Dennis's favorite meal was liver and onions.

Good, I thought. I knew how to make that. I'd grown up on liver and onions and I cooked a meal that I knew was a winner. Sabotaged by Pastor Banks, it turned out that Dennis totally *hated* this one meal. Dinner was very awkward, with Dennis pushing the food around the plate to avoid the liver. He ate the vegetables, but I could tell he wasn't enjoying his meal. This was a totally new experience for me, because I can cook. I mean, I can *really* cook! I had never had anybody eat my food and not rave about it.

Not only did Dennis hate the meal, he also didn't stay long after. And I didn't hear from him for about two months. I guess he really did hate liver and onions. The distance stung at first. My ego was hurt more than anything else. But I just moved on with my life. I'd see him in church occasionally, but we'd just exchange cordial greetings and nothing more.

Still, I couldn't stop thinking about him. But there was no way I was chasing after any man. I decided if he never talked to me again, I would get over it and move on. I was in a place of indifference, which was a great place for me to be at this point in my life, as a single woman.

From November to February, Dennis and I would see each

other at church, we greeted one another, and that was it. I thought to myself that the "voice," the epiphany, must have been my imagination.

A few more months passed, and I closed on my first home. Having my own home was a dream come true. I found this beautiful house in an all-white neighborhood. It was a stone house with four bedrooms and two full bathrooms. It was close to my job, and cost $33,000.

What I loved the most about this house was the stone fireplace and the landscape. Beautiful azaleas surrounded the house, and there were lush trees in the front and back of the house. It was breathtaking in the fall and spring. The house had been built by one of the energy engineers at the plant. My boss at the plant knew the first owner of the home and told me that the house would be a good buy for me.

My utility bills were almost nothing because the house had more than the normal inches of insulation. And the trees provided great shade in hot summer months. The house also had a screened porch and window providing access to the outdoor grill, which I used often to prepare whatever new recipe I was trying out from my father's kitchen.

After I closed on the house and moved in, I invited a bunch of my friends and most of the church over for a housewarming. Dennis came. My mother came and she was all up in his face about whether he was dating me. I had stupidly told my sister Cookie about the vision I'd had so many months ago.

The one that said Dennis would be the man I would marry. I should have known Cookie couldn't keep anything to herself and would share it with my mother.

Mother really wanted me to get married—to anyone, at this point. Here I was with this big house and no one to share it with. In her mind, that was not a pretty picture. This wasn't a celebration for her, but a reminder that I was digging in for the long haul as an old maid.

For me, however, my life was very full. I had plenty of men to date, who would take me to the movies, dinner, or wherever else I wanted to go. I was having fun. Yes, I wanted to get married and start a family. But I decided to stop being so overwhelmed about being single at my age—I had to trust God with that. I was going to just live my life and not settle for anything or anybody who didn't love me the way I wanted to be loved.

So while my mother was very interested in Dennis Meredith, I wasn't really paying him much attention at my housewarming party. The woman he was dating and had broken up with (numerous times) came too. They came separately and left separately. I didn't make much of that, either.

The next time I saw Dennis was during choir rehearsal later that week. I was always cutting up in choir rehearsal, cracking jokes and having fun. I was popular in the choir. But Dennis was the star of the choir. That man could sing. He was also a television news photographer. Since I needed someone to fix my TV, which was acting up, I asked him to come over and take a look at it if he had time.

I also wanted to see if it was the liver and onions or me that kept him away. I wanted culinary vindication. This time when he came over, I had something different waiting for him—my famous fried fish. My daddy would send me meats and fish that I kept in a deep freezer. I had thawed out some whiting earlier and fried it up.

When he came in, I offered him something to eat. The smell alone was enough to make any person with taste buds weak. He didn't talk much during this meal either, other than to utter an occasional "Wow!" He ate and ate and ate. After he ate until he was full, he came up for air and we finally started talking, which we did for the rest of the night. I don't think he ever did look at my broken television. Before he left, he stopped at the front door and kissed me. Fireworks went off inside my head. I had never experienced a kiss like that. And the voice that had told me that I would be marrying Dennis Meredith was back, confirming, "He is the one."

We started spending more and more time together. One afternoon, I was playing tennis with a Sunday school student I was mentoring. Dennis dropped by the courts and asked me to drive him someplace. We ended up at a motorcycle dealership. He bought a bike and followed me home on it. We went riding the rest of the day. This was the first time I had ever been on a motorcycle, but I felt completely safe. Dennis's father, "Big

June," who was a member of a Harley-Davidson biker's club, had taught Dennis how to ride at a young age, and he was a pro. And with Dennis's height and size, he just seemed invincible. I was never worried.

Dennis started coming by every day to eat, and sometimes we would go riding afterward or go play tennis, or basketball, or some other fun thing. We went everywhere on that motorcycle. We even rode to Chattanooga for Memorial Day to visit my sister Mina. Mina (Wilhelmina) and her husband, Rock (Calvin Moore), had been married since graduating college and owned a house with a swimming pool. We ate barbecue and went swimming and came back the next day on the bike. It was so much fun.

I didn't even think about being scared or the potential danger—it was just so thrilling riding on that bike.

Dennis knew how to have fun. I enjoyed being with him. Our relationship at this point was just about having fun with each other. He said he didn't want to get into anything serious. "We're just hanging out," Dennis said. I was fine with that. I didn't really want a serious relationship either. Even with that voice telling me that this man would be my husband, I figured if that was going to happen, it would. I wasn't pressing it. I was enjoying getting to know him as a friend. And we were becoming good friends. Dennis was so honest with me. He would tell me things that most men wouldn't tell a woman.

He told me that the reason he didn't want to get serious

with me was because he was a dog. He said he couldn't be trusted. "I don't even trust myself half the time," he said. I guess when people tell you who they are, believe them! But none of that mattered to me then, because we were "just friends." I was simply enjoying his company.

We dated casually into the summer. His family reunion was in August. He didn't have a car, just a motorcycle, and Toledo was too far to travel on a bike. I had Sadie. She was a jalopy, but she got us to his family reunion in Toledo and back. The previous year, he had taken the other girl to meet his family. His family was nice to her. But before we left the reunion, his mother told him that I was the one.

Dennis's family was a big, tight-knit family like mine, with strong traditions that held the family together despite drama. His father was hardworking and had worked in a foundry after leaving the army, where he served in the Korean War. He carried a pistol, rode a Harley-Davidson, and was in a motorcycle club: no one messed with Eddie "Big June" Meredith. He was a tough man, but he loved his family and provided for them. He understood this to be the only indicator of love required.

He went to work every day, never missing a day, just like my dad. He worked for Unicast Foundry all of his life and retired from there. He also lost his good health there. He contracted lung disease. That he chain-smoked Lucky Strikes didn't help matters.

He was a tough man, ready to take on anyone, with his pistol or fist, who would physically or verbally threaten his family. (Second indicator of his love.) He had learned this from his father, and his father had learned this from his father. He was not an affectionate man and was "easily" provoked. Don't mess up playing bid whist and play the wrong card; he would say his usual "Got damn it!" and shake his head.

Marital physical fights started from escalating small arguments coupled with drinking. Weekend and holiday drinking would always lead to family drama. Food was a big deal for the Meredith family. The Meredith men were big eaters. Dennis's grandmother was a great cook, and weekly and holiday family gatherings were the tradition of the family and everybody was expected to be present.

Dennis's mother, Osie Lee Taylor, whom I called Mom, had an awesome personality. She was an only child, but not spoiled. We loved each other the moment we set eyes on each other.

The family attended Calvary Baptist Church and were strong supporters of it. Big June was not a churchgoer but a believer who attended "radio church" in the comfort of his living room. He loved to listen to Rev. C. L. Franklin preaching on Sunday morning while he prepared Sunday dinner for the family returning from church.

He taught Dennis at an early age that if Dennis was going to be a "believable" preacher, he should preach from his heart, not use a script, and that he should have a strong "hoop" (music) at the end of the sermon, just like Rev. C. L. Franklin.

For June, if you had to have a script to preach, you were fake and not called by God.

I had a great time in Ohio. It felt like home. And while we were still just friends, hanging out and having fun, I was grateful that he had invited me.

Right after we got back, Dennis said, "I think we need to pray about getting married." I was in shock. He had been the one saying he didn't want to get serious. I had put myself in a whole different kind of mind-set. "Fun only" was where I was with him. Now he was talking about praying to get married?

The day we were supposed to pray, Dennis called and said he had changed his mind. I was crushed. I broke down crying. That night, I took a shower and I prayed. I prayed for God to take away the emotions and any feelings I had for Dennis, which were growing by the day. I couldn't do the roller coaster. It was just too much. When I got up from my knees, there was a knock at my front door. It was Dennis.

He was standing there looking sad. I had just fixed dinner before he canceled. He now was in love with my cooking (after that liver debacle, of course). I invited him in to eat. We didn't talk much through the meal. After dinner, we were sitting on this black lounger and he told me he was going home to wash his hair. He had a small 'fro and his hair was thin. I told him to let me scratch his head. I used to scratch my daddy's head often before he went to bed.

Dennis took a seat on the floor between my legs as I parted

his hair and scratched his scalp. He was acting like he was dozing off, and I leaned over and kissed him on his forehead when I was done. Before I could sit up, he grabbed my face with both of his hands and kissed me full on the mouth passionately. I could hardly catch my breath. All I was thinking was, *Okay, let's do it!*

He looked at me and said, "Do I have to beg?"

I said, "No, but I hope you have a condom."

He did and we did it. It was great. It was better than great. It was so good I finally understood what all of the fuss was about. I finally got it. And I wanted to do it again and again and again. And we did.

After a night of passion, we finally prayed together. That weekend we got engaged. We set a date for December 3, 1978.

CHAPTER FOUR

I Do!

When I brought Dennis Andrew Meredith home, you would have thought I brought Jesus home. My parents knew he was a minister, and they had great respect for ministers. Our family took care of every preacher that served as pastor at our home church—I believe today this is one of the reasons that our family was blessed in the midst of being so poor. Nonetheless, Daddy and Mother loved Dennis.

While the Mitcham clan was pleased, not many of our

church family at Sardis was as pleased with our announcement.

People in our church were shocked to learn that Dennis
and I were getting married. They couldn't believe that Dennis
had asked me to marry him. I was not at all what people had
imagined for him. And I was definitely not first-lady material
for a pastor, let alone one as well put together and sharp as
Dennis.

I was not a typical church girl. And I wasn't even the kind
of woman Dennis normally dated or who was waiting in line
for him to ask her out.

Ellen, the woman Dennis was dating when I met him, was
perfection. Her hair was perfect—I mean, not one strand was
out of place. It was like they'd cut her out of a magazine. She
was picture-perfect. She looked like a young Diahann Carroll.

I was boyish, loud, and crass. I loved to laugh, and when I
laughed, I laughed loudly and boldly. I said whatever I wanted
to say. I worked with men, some really rough men, and they
didn't intimidate me at all. I guess I was a feminist in an era
when women in my community were not feminist.

I had a woman in the church have the nerve to ask me if I
wore panties.

"That's none of your business," I said.

That day, I had on my tiny tennis skirt, and my legs were
beautiful from tennis and swimming. I guess she wanted to
know.

Another reason people were shocked was because we had kept our relationship a secret. Remember, in the beginning we were just hanging out as friends, nothing serious. So when we announced the engagement everybody was thinking, *He's marrying* her?

They all thought he would end up with Ellen. But he wasn't happy with her. She was always comparing him to Pastor Banks. She was really close to Pastor Banks and she would say to Dennis, "Why don't you do this like Pastor Banks?" She wanted to mold Dennis into another Pastor Banks.

Pastor Banks was freaking out about our engagement. He didn't like Dennis for me at all. I never knew why, but he thought Dennis would be a horrible mate for me. (Remember when he tried to sabotage our first date by suggesting I serve Dennis liver and onions?) I totaled Sadie not long after our engagement, and Pastor said it was a sign from God not to marry Dennis. Of course, I ignored him.

I didn't care who didn't want us to get married. I was excited about it. I wasn't, however, excited about the prospect of an actual wedding. I wanted to get married, but I didn't want a big to-do of a ceremony. But once people got over their shock, they wouldn't hear of anything but a big wedding. All of the Sardis church ladies got together and conspired to throw me the biggest, best wedding ever.

I had tried to set the table for what I wanted. I told everyone I wanted something small, intimate, with not a whole lot of drama. I didn't want to spend a whole lot of money, either. So when a few months passed and the ladies in the church started asking me what I was going to do, my response was: "Nothing."

One of the church ladies owned a floral shop and she said she wanted to pitch in. I told her I didn't have much money to spend on a wedding. She told me she would provide the flowers to me for free! Many people in the church just started pitching in—friends and family alike.

I was (and still am) very frugal. My mind does not work the way most people's minds work. I do not believe people should invest in nice cars and live in "rented" apartments. I believe in buying assets (property that appreciates in value)—and not buying liabilities—cars are liabilities: the minute you drive it off the lot the value drops by thousands. So, I meant it when I said that I wasn't paying for a wedding. But so many folks in Sardis came forward to volunteer to do things for free. The wedding ended up being grander than I could ever have imagined.

Someone made us some beautiful programs. Dennis's mother took care of the dresses for the flower girls and the tuxedo for the ring bearer.

We had twelve bridesmaids and twelve groomsmen. My sisters made all of the bridesmaids' dresses. The music was free—we were both part of the church's music ministry, so that was easy. And we had tons of volunteers, including thirty hostesses. It was unbelievable, and I was so appreciative.

I had eight sisters, and seven of them were in my wedding. Our families traveled from Macon, Georgia, and Toledo, Ohio, to Birmingham, and my family took over my house. I stayed with Angie, who was one of my bridesmaids. Dennis's whole church from Toledo was there. My church family from Macon was there too. There were so many people staying at my house, it was crazy. Even some of the hostesses from Sardis had to take in some of my people for the weekend. Dennis's and my family members were scattered all over town, staying with different members of our church. It was beautiful to see how loved we were, so much so that people would just open their homes and donate their time and talent to make our day special.

As the day drew near, I started to get petrified. I wasn't used to all of this attention. I actually hated being the center of attention. I was an emotional wreck. I would cry at the drop of a hat. So I disappeared for a while. I went to my campus and just hid out there. I had enrolled in a continuing education program at the University of Alabama in Birmingham. I had just finished a computer exam. I was always in school for something. I had to study. I wanted to study—to do anything but think about this wedding.

I was so immersed in my studies that I missed my own wedding shower. My sisters and girlfriends were livid. But I used school as an excuse for getting out of all of the pomp and circumstance and chaos that went with planning a wedding.

That just wasn't my thing. They went ahead and had the shower anyway. They had it without me. I had so many gifts. It was overwhelming and amazing. I could not believe this was happening to me. I just showed up. There was a dress waiting for me—a beautiful dress that fit perfectly.

People volunteered to photograph the festivities. Dennis's grandmother hosted the rehearsal dinner and cooked all the food. My daddy ranted and raved over the food. He said, "*This* woman can cook." That was a high compliment, coming from him.

I don't even remember the rehearsal, I was so excited and out of sorts. I barely remember the wedding itself. I was in a dream state. I do remember a few things about the wedding. One was how beautiful the church looked. The wedding ended up being on a first Sunday. And when I set foot in the church I couldn't believe my eyes. The woman with the flower shop had transformed it into an elaborate tabernacle. It was something you'd see in a movie—simply beautiful, with flowers and candles everywhere. The church looked like a candlelit garden. And it was packed that Sunday like it had never been before.

We had communion service at the altar with both my pastor and Dennis's pastor officiating. The joy of my heart that day was my father walking me down the aisle to release me to my husband-to-be and hearing Dennis singing the song he wrote for me:

I was a long way from home, with no one to call my own;
  then I found you.
I didn't know at the time that you were gonna be mine,
  but now it's true.
God has destined every man to fit his master plan.
Look what God has done—since I made up my mind
I know that God is on my side.

After thirty-plus years I can still remember that first verse. I was wearing little makeup, but after that song I had none left. And the entire church was also in tears.

At the reception, all I remember was sitting on my daddy's lap and hugging him tightly. I was so happy.

"You know, Dennis needs to get his own church, because he preaches way better than Pastor Banks," my daddy said.

The year before, when I had brought Dennis down to Macon to meet my parents, my daddy had loved him immediately. This was strange, because my daddy had barely spoken two words to the last man I brought home. It was "Hey!" and then my daddy walked off. It was the same when I brought Paul, a premed student, home; and the same with Rick, who graduated from Mercer, and went on to become an airline pilot. My daddy didn't say anything to him, either. But with Dennis, Daddy couldn't stop talking and laughing with him.

Dennis just fit right in. He started to play the piano and my daddy was impressed. He said to me, "You need to get that man a piano." Realizing that pastors didn't make a lot of money, he knew that Dennis couldn't afford one. My daddy also said, "Well, you ain't never going to have that much, but you'll always have plenty to eat, because they always feed the preacher."

I didn't need Dennis's money. I made lots of money—especially for a woman back then. And I wasn't a spender. So our finances would be fine.

I was making about $1,300 a month at U.S. Steel. In the late 1970s and early 1980s, this was considered very good money. Dennis never showed any kind of male chauvinism. In fact, right after we got married, I put his name on the deed to my house and got us joint accounts.

He was making a little more than minimum wage at his day job as a TV news photographer for Channel 13 and received no pay as the youth pastor at Sardis. Sometimes he would make $15 to $50 when he preached at special occasions and revivals. Whatever he made, he brought it to me. He loved to spend. If it were up to Dennis, he'd have had a new car every year. He was the ultimate consumer and I was the consummate saver. We were really opposites. He lived for recreation time and I lived to work.

But it worked. We worked. During our first couple of years, we did everything together. We were like glue—together 24/7.

I noticed, however, a little time into our marriage that

Dennis's demeanor was changing. He wasn't as happy as he was when we first got married. I called Dennis at his job one day and he wasn't there. That was very unusual. I left my job, worried, and found him at home in bed.

"Why are you not at work?" I asked him. "You're not sick."

He said he was depressed. He hated his job and didn't want to go back.

"So why don't you go back to school and get your seminary degree?" I suggested.

He had finished high school and gone to college for a semester and dropped out. He'd done better than the rest of his family, who simply had high school diplomas. The tradition was to finish high school and go work in a factory for thirty years and then retire. That meant you had made it in the Meredith family.

In my family, that would be unacceptable. Everybody went to college. We were all groomed to go to college. We didn't have a choice. So it was natural for me to suggest that Dennis go back to school. I couldn't stay out of school; I was always adding more degrees and certifications.

He called his mother and told her what I'd suggested.

"Go for it," she said. "I have nothing to do with what y'all are doing down there."

So Dennis quit his job. We got a loan for the first year and he had a scholarship for the other three years. I filled out the enrollment package and the applications for all the scholarships and I was able to secure one from the Southern Baptists. I don't think we paid for more than one semester. And I made enough to cover all of that.

A little while after Dennis started school, we found out that we were having a baby. We went out to dinner after work one night, and I started to feel faint. I was accustomed to not eating much—although I do love to eat. I would sometimes be so busy that I'd forget to eat. I imagined I was light-headed because I hadn't eaten enough that day. But Dennis was concerned and insisted that I go to the doctor the next day. I did. They ran a pregnancy test, and to my surprise it came back positive. Dennis was already madly in love with me, but with this news I became the absolute center of his universe. I was carrying his firstborn child.

He had been nudging me since we got married to have a baby. I was pushing thirty and Dennis had his own pressures.

"I've got to have some kids for the family reunion," he said.

His family reunion was a real big deal every year. He had three brothers and they all had kids—all boys. He was the only one without kids. And boys ran in the family. Big June was one of five boys, no girls. And Dennis had no sisters.

It took me a long time to show any signs of pregnancy. I didn't need maternity clothes until the sixth month. But after that sixth month, it was if I was nine months pregnant overnight.

Dennis's career as a preacher was taking off. He was becoming quite popular as he honed his preaching skills in school. Churches all over the country were starting to request him more frequently to guest preach. He was out of town a lot during my pregnancy. But Dennis made sure that his mother would come down to stay with me, to look after and pamper me the way he pampered me.

Every evening after dinner, Dennis would run me a bath or massage my feet and rub my belly. He made sure I was eating right. And he wouldn't let me do any work around the house.

When Dennis's mother, whom I called Mom, came to stay, she would have dinner ready every evening when I got home from work. Yes, I worked right up until the delivery date. After dinner, I would insist that Mom and I go for a walk. I couldn't play tennis, but I still craved exercise. While returning from one of our walks I said, "Mom, I don't think I can get any bigger!" I was about eight months pregnant and feeling pretty uncomfortable.

"Sweetie, you ain't seen nothing yet," she said, smiling.

I didn't believe her. But she was right. Within a few weeks, I was wobbling here and there. I could barely walk. I had only gained twenty-five pounds during the entire pregnancy, but I felt as if I was carrying the Incredible Hulk.

As I waited for the baby to come, I found myself sitting at home bored for two weeks after the actual delivery date. The baby refused to come. My sister Mina came down to help me. As she waited for the baby to come, she took time to decorate our nursery, creating the most beautiful baby room imaginable. Mina could sew her butt off, and she made cushions for the rocker that matched the curtains. It looked amazing. Dennis painted the room and bought a few things for the baby too. That nursery was a good indication of how spoiled this baby would be when he actually arrived.

Dennis was so attentive during my pregnancy and the actual birth. He was a pillar of strength for me because I was so very scared. I knew it was going to hurt. I hate pain. He attended Lamaze classes with me and we would simulate contractions and do all of the breathing. He was the one coaching me and getting everything perfect.

I was so uncomfortable in my ninth month it was almost unbearable. I couldn't find any spot where I could get any rest. I was still swimming, and that seemed to help a little. And I didn't really put on any weight. Outside of having this big old belly, I carried on as if I wasn't even pregnant. But as the delivery date drew near, I got more anxious.

The night I went into labor, Dennis was studying in another room. My water broke around eight in the evening. I called out to Dennis and he came running. I started to cry. He said, "Why are you crying?"

"I know I'm getting ready to hurt really bad!" I said through my tears.

Dennis just smiled. He was so excited. He had packed my bag a week before. We got to the hospital and he dressed in the scrubs and was right there. I was in so much pain, as I'd predicted I would be. My contractions were one minute apart, and I hadn't dilated one centimeter. The doctor discovered that I wasn't opening up. The baby was lodged up under my breasts. He was so content in my tummy that he was determined not to come out.

Dennis was holding my hand as my doctor told me, "We're going to have to do a cesarean because the baby won't drop." They prepped me for a different kind of delivery and drew my blood. That was when Dennis checked out. He fainted. Passed out.

"Get him out of here!" the doctor said.

They had to carry Dennis out of the room. So he ended up missing the actual birth. Our first baby was born November 14, 1979. We named him Dennis Taylor Meredith, II. But we called him Taylor, which was Dennis's mother's maiden name. She was an only child and we wanted to keep her family name alive.

Dennis's mother came and stayed with me for a week after I gave birth. Dennis's grandmother came and stayed with us for a while too. And my mother came and stayed with me for a week as well. Someone was always with me. When Dennis wasn't there with me, either his mother was there or his grandmother was there. Dennis was preaching revivals during this time, but I was never alone.

Taylor was barely a month old when we started traveling with him. We had to take him to Toledo to see Dennis's family, of course. We drove ten hours. And Taylor was perfect the whole trip—mostly clinging to my breast. I enjoyed the connection while nursing him. Another benefit was that for the first time in my life I had full breasts.

In Toledo, he was spoiled rotten. Everybody just doted on him.

When we got back, we were to introduce Taylor to the church family. While I was in the hospital having Taylor, Dennis had bought me a suit, with a hat, gloves, and shoes to match for the occasion. He told me I had four weeks to fit into this outfit, which he proudly spread out onto the bed when I returned home from the hospital.

"This is how I want you to look when you go back to church," he said.

I was back to my normal weight in four weeks and that outfit fit perfectly. I wore it with pride when Taylor got blessed at Sardis—the purse, the gloves, the shoes, the suit. Everything was perfect. I never had to shop for myself. Every nice thing in my closet, Dennis bought. He loved to dress me. And I didn't mind.

"Lydia, you need to start wearing makeup," he would say to me from time to time if we were going somewhere special. I didn't wear makeup normally. But again, I didn't mind wearing it for him. So I started wearing makeup. When you love someone, it's not hard to do the things they ask you to do.

I was back to work in eight weeks—because I was so bored.

I had never taken off one day from work before I got pregnant, except for my honeymoon. I had built up so much sick time and vacation time that I got paid the entire time I was out on maternity leave.

I had enough time saved up that I could have stayed out for the whole year. But I didn't. I couldn't wait to get back to work. The babysitter lived in the neighborhood. I would come home on my lunch break and nurse my baby and go back to work. I had good babysitters, mostly from the church. They helped out so much.

Everything was on track for a while. Dennis was deep into his studies. He was making all As and Bs and they loved him at the university. During his junior year, he said he was tired, and was taking time off.

"You're too close to the end," I told him. "You have to finish."

I got the pastors and some of his mentors to call him and encourage him to keep going. Pastor Banks was the one who actually swayed him to finish, which he did. He was back on track to graduate. And around this time, I found out I was pregnant again!

CHAPTER FIVE

First Lady Meredith

While I was juggling work and motherhood, the last thing on my mind was becoming first lady of a church. But as Dennis got closer to graduation, that thought was becoming a reality. I was ill-prepared for the experience.

I was raised in the church, just as many black people were in my generation. My parents were devoted to the church. They took care of the pastor and his wife until they died. Then the next first family came in and they took care of them until they died—taking them food and making sure they were okay, and giving them respect and care.

Mother kept us in line and taught us to respect the leaders of the church. When we were little, she used to tell us a story of kids who made fun of a preacher and were eaten by bears. She tried to scare us into acting right with the preacher and his wife, and it worked. The pastor was right, no matter what. Even when he wasn't right.

As I mentioned, our first lady was one of the meanest people I ever knew. She was tall and thin and wore glasses that made her look intelligent. She wore dresses that came down to her ankles. But what made her unattractive was her consistently mean, arrogant, and pious attitude.

First Lady Johnson was in the choir, but she couldn't sing a lick. Being in the choir was the only service that I saw her do. She never did anything but occasionally mess up the choir, sit in her seat, ride in her Cadillac, and wear her new clothes.

She was not someone you went up to and gave a hug. I don't remember her even shaking anyone's hand. Her body language, her countenance, was just stern. She seemed to be miserable, in church, every Sunday.

I never aspired to be a first lady of a church, especially growing up with Mrs. Johnson as my first lady. All I thought was, *Her life certainly isn't full of joy.* And who wanted to live like that?

I didn't understand the strain and stress and all the things a woman who was married to a pastor might have to deal with until I married a preacher and ended up being thrust into that role.

Dennis became the pastor of Mount Zion Missionary Baptist Church during his junior year at Samford University. It was a midsize church in East Thomas—a predominantly poor community in Birmingham. This church would be the first of many churches we served in poverty-stricken communities.

As I mentioned, I never wanted to marry a minister. And I definitely never imagined serving in the role of first lady, especially given my tactless, graceless demeanor and ambition to become affluent and successful in my own right. First ladies of my day were trophy pieces and very traditional. They stood by their men and were gentle spirits who didn't have an opinion. If they did, they never gave it.

Just as I never wanted to be a first lady, ironically, Dennis never wanted to be the pastor of his own church. He was content as an assistant or youth pastor. But I pushed him, challenging him to go to school and aspire for more. I wanted him to reach his full potential. I believed in Dennis. His talent was phenomenal. Even my daddy told Dennis that he needed his own church.

We weren't the only ones who felt that way. We later found out that Mrs. Taylor, a good friend of the family who frequently invited us to Sunday dinner after church, recommended Dennis to Mount Zion. Mrs. Taylor was a longtime member of Sardis and was one of the hostesses at our wedding.

Mrs. Taylor gave Dennis's name to the chairman of the pulpit committee, who was also chairman of the deacon board at Mount Zion. At the urging of Mrs. Taylor, Dennis submitted his résumé to become their pastor. He had been a guest preacher there, and had sung his behind off there as well.

I had just gotten home from work and was unwinding when the phone rang. Dennis was working late at the church, preparing for a youth event we were having that Sunday. It was Mr. Loomis from the deacon board at Mount Zion. I took the opportunity to tell him what a great man, father, husband, and preacher Dennis was.

"I'm calling because your husband is a leading candidate," Deacon Loomis said. "But don't brag so much."

I guess I was so excited. I couldn't wait for Dennis to get home to tell him. When he walked in the door, I gave him a big hug.

"I think this is it," I told him. "You will have your church."

The following week, Dennis had an interview with all of the decision makers at the church, and that Sunday he was the guest preacher again.

When he stepped into the pulpit, it was clear to me and everyone else in that congregation that Dennis Meredith would be their next pastor.

I was in my last month of pregnancy with our second child

when they called Dennis and offered him the job. I was scheduled for another C-section the same week he was scheduled to start. Taylor stayed with Mrs. Taylor while we went to the hospital. I told Taylor's primary caregiver (Lula Pugh, who worked at the Sardis Day Care) that Taylor needed to be potty-trained a couple of months before my due date—because there was no way I could handle two babies in diapers. And he was. Taylor was always developmentally ahead for his age. Even before his baby brother was born, he cooperated to help, protect, and provide for his brother. He still does!

Dennis and I were excited about this baby. We both wanted a girl. For me, that would be it. One boy! One girl! Mommy and Daddy! Completion! But God had other plans.

Micah Devin Meredith was born February 11, 1981.

He came into the world relatively quietly. The C-section went well. Dennis didn't faint. And we delivered the most beautiful child I had ever seen. Dennis agreed.

"Look how beautiful he is," he said, beaming with pride.

Micah was such a pleasant and peaceful child. Dennis now had two sons to show off at the next family reunion.

I was once again anxious to get back to work. I followed my doctor's instructions to the letter and breastfed, just as I had done with Taylor. I dropped all the weight I had gained (which wasn't much) within four weeks after the birth. And again, Dennis bought me an outfit to wear at Micah's baby dedication service, which would be at our new church, Mount Zion.

Shortly after the baby dedication, they had an installation ceremony for Dennis at Mount Zion. It was a beautiful ceremony with many dynamic guest speakers. Dennis's family came from Toledo and mine came from Macon. Even Reverend Banks from Sardis was there to see him installed.

Reverend Banks hadn't been very supportive of Dennis pastoring his own church. Nor had he been very supportive of our relationship. Perhaps he knew something. Or maybe he was sad to see some of the biggest tithers in his church leave. My salary continued to grow because I was still a top performer at work and got raises annually.

But Reverend Banks was there and brought most of Sardis with him to see Dennis installed. Even classmates and professors—including his favorite, Dr. Crowley—from Dennis's school came as well.

We were officially Pastor and First Lady Meredith of the Mount Zion Baptist Church. I would soon find out that "first lady" was not a coveted seat, and I would begin to learn my first lessons about church folk and how churches really operated.

At Sardis, Dennis and I had been laypeople. We volunteered our services. Dennis had grown the youth ministry and I was in the choir, but we were never involved with the politics of the church. We were never the primary object of attention or gossip; we were not the "first family."

Being in leadership at our first church assignment, we

found that some members were very cautious and sometimes contemptible in their efforts to protect the church from anything they thought Dennis would do. Some people simply do not like change—even for the better. Then you had the members whose whole motive for being in church was to be seen and to get praise from the pastor and other members. Most "be-seen" members like this would come and go.

Some members thrived on gossip, and the pastor's family was the center of the gossip syndicate. Most "gossiping" members were there to create and feed on church drama. Some members were the "stab you in the back, throw the rock, hide their hands" kind of folk. These members wore at least two faces, and you'd never know what face to expect.

There were members who never stirred up drama and were strong volunteers but refused to financially support the ministry. Some members would give financial support but would not volunteer to support any programs. As Dennis's wife, sometimes I felt resented for just being his wife.

There were very few members you could count on to volunteer, to give, and to edify the church, to keep the church ministry growing and thriving. But sadly, they were not in the majority.

Dennis has always looked to see the best in the worst-behaving folks—taking parishioners at their word. To his credit, he always tried to love and protect the Mount Zion congregation.

Dennis only made $125 a week as pastor at Mount Zion. Most pastors were expected to have second jobs, but Dennis wanted to work full-time at the church. I agreed with this approach. I made enough money to supplement his salary and provide for our growing family, which allowed Dennis to finish his final year of school with flying colors.

Dennis went into ministry full speed ahead. The physical condition of the church was immaculate, so he started immediately trying to improve the delivery of worship to increase church membership and income. He brought in a new church organist who was super talented and hardworking to start building the music ministry of the church, which left a lot to be desired. With the revamped choir and music ministry coupled with Dennis's preaching, the pristine, beautiful church was soon packed every Sunday.

Mount Zion took good care of the church. And it was perfectly located—right around the corner from where I'd learned how to swim. Mount Zion seated a hundred and fifty comfortably, with another fifty in the choir stand.

The trustees and deacons ran the church. The pastor had zero control over church business. His job was to preach. That was it. The trustees and deacons would have leadership meetings often—sometimes at their homes and sometimes at the church, regardless of the location—dinner would always be served. I looked forward to these dinners, because these women could cook! And I loved to eat. My daddy's observation, that the church would always feed the preacher even if they couldn't pay him much, turned out to be true. With parenting two young children, working full-time (and now Dennis was too), having help with meal preparation was truly a blessing!

Despite the cold shoulder I was receiving from some of the members, I rolled up my sleeves and got involved relatively quickly in the affairs of the church. I started hosting Bible study and joined the choir. Unlike the first lady from my childhood church, I could actually carry a tune.

I kept a low profile at Mount Zion. Besides the pleasure of enjoying a delicious, home cooked meal for my entire family (that I didn't have to shop for or prepare), another church activity that gave me great joy was singing in the choir. I always enjoyed the choir. I was in church choirs most of my life.

There were maybe five families out of the whole congregation with whom I connected. Soon, some members started to warm up to me. A few were even kind. Mrs. Finney, who owned a restaurant and was wealthy, told me where to shop for my suits. I needed to be well dressed as first lady.

"I have a store credit there," she told me. "Please feel free to use it."

There are always one or two families in every church who have plenty of money. There was one other family that was nice to me, the Fraziers. Both Sarah and Walter could really sing. Sarah babysat Taylor and Micah and we became very close. She would prepare meals in the evening and our family would go over to the Fraziers most evenings for dinner. It was a real help.

Most of the congregation, however, were indifferent and ignored me. And those who were just plain mean I dealt with the way my mother, Annie Mae, taught me—I killed them with kindness and humor. Soon the antagonism began to melt away. I never returned those nasty looks or responded to the comments that I wasn't supposed to hear but were spoken loud enough for me to hear.

These people seemed to scrutinize everything about me, but I didn't care what they thought about me; having been raised in the Mitcham household had cured me of being sensitive. You had to have thick skin to survive living with my mother and sisters. The only person whose opinion about me mattered was Dennis's. I let him dress me and make suggestions here and there about my appearance. He always wanted me to look beautiful. So he took me shopping for clothes, the right shoes, and makeup. He even taught me how to apply makeup because I'd never really worn it before. Dennis also made sure I got my hair pressed and curled every week.

This was a real upgrade from the Afro, jeans, and hard hat I wore to work, or the tennis skirt I was prone to be wearing on any given week day after work. I actually enjoyed the makeover. The transition was nice. I enjoyed looking and feeling beautiful. I never knew how addictive this could be until I became an ex–first lady.

I dressed the part. But I still didn't fully act the part.

I didn't sit with my legs daintily crossed on the first pew with a fan and a prayer cloth across my lap, looking for the congregation to adore me. I wasn't quiet and perfect, smiling lovingly at my husband as he delivered his fiery sermon. I didn't wear elaborate hats. I did wear a hat every Sunday, but it was always very tasteful and understated, a bold contrast to my personality.

Most first ladies whom I came in contact with were very timid and passive women. They did just what their husbands told them to do. You could spot a first lady in a congregation a mile away—by what she wore, where she sat, and how she carried herself. I never observed any of these women taking leadership in their husband's churches, or serving in their communities. They were primarily window dressing.

I was a working first lady. When Dennis was hired at his next church in California, I was still making the majority of the family money as an engineer. By then, he too was making good money and we were thriving as a family. In addition to contributing my tithe, I always pitched in—helping to build the church so that he could concentrate on winning souls. Later, I even gave up my career and the money that went with it to totally support his dream as I worked as a secretary in the church office, planning and organizing and managing.

For most of my years as first lady, if I wasn't working eighty-plus hours a week outside the church to make sure our family made ends meet, I was working eighty-plus hours a week inside the church, making sure the lights stayed on and things ran smoothly. At our last church, I even established a successful child-care facility and community outreach program.

This wasn't my plan; this was God's plan. This was the enterprise that God had given me to run. It was the business that I had envisioned so many years before. And I loved it. I loved it so much that I'm still running a child-care facility and school to this day.

Back then, Dennis was a devoted husband, a present father. He was working hard in school, and I was going to be there for him no matter what.

He was the first in his family to finish college and the first to work with something other than his hands. Most of the men in his family were laborers, working a job from sunup to sundown, getting drunk and running around with women on the weekends, and going back to work on Monday morning. The ritual continued until they were too old to drink and run around with women and retired.

My father and mother were laborers too. But they envisioned their ten children having lives much different from their own, free from the arduous work they endured. They pushed us to complete college—which all ten of us did! Some of us even have advanced degrees. We didn't have much money growing up, but because my parents were hell-bent on making our lives better, they disciplined us harshly to be good citizens and make good grades in school. The outcome was that we all earned full scholarships to college. I never let go of my dream of owning my own business and serving God. The latter part of that vision was most important in my family. That's what we saw our parents do—serve God and people. All my life, I saw them giving back and helping folks less fortunate than we were.

Running or owning a business and helping the poor were not the primary roles of a first lady of a church. I had no role models or mentors to consult when I was thrust into that position. Dennis would always tell me that I should go to the Baptist Church and Bible conventions they would have four times a year across the country with him and attend the classes in the women's division so I could network and learn. I went to one. The teacher was a black pastor whose message was that we should expect our husbands to be unfaithful if we were fat and out of shape. That was the last class I went to. I decided I would figure it out on my own. I pioneered my own way.

And Dennis did too. He wasn't traditional. He was very charismatic and had his own ideas about how he was going to do things, but some church leaders weren't willing to bend. Dennis got into a big fight at Mount Zion with some of the deacons and trustees. It was kind of contentious. And it was soon time to leave.

After he graduated from college, Dennis had applied to a Southern Baptist seminary in California. We prayed to test God's will for us to leave Alabama. Every prayer was answered. We sold the piano that I'd bought for Dennis as my daddy had demanded; Dennis was accepted into one of the most prestigious seminaries in the nation, Golden Gate Baptist Theological Seminary; and we were able to sell the house in the middle of the worst recession the city had ever experienced. Where I worked at U.S. Steel–Fairfield Works was now a ghost town, with 16,000 workers laid off. (I was not laid off because I programmed computers at one of the newer plants still running, but I decided that I would have a stronger corporate future working in a different industry where foreign market competition would not cause it to crumble. I chose the industry of energy and landed a job with Southern Company.)

Because we believed that God was leading us to move to California, we began to make plans. I mailed twenty résumés to the San Francisco Bay Area. I was confident I could find work because of Affirmative Action—being black and a female. I was surprised and disappointed with only one month left before the move: I had received twenty rejections to the twenty résumés. We decided that we would live off of the proceeds of the house sale until I found employment, but we also knew that this money would not last very long. Dennis boldly told me to resign my job in Alabama anyway. I had only been working at Southern Company for a year, and they had invested a lot in my training. But I was obedient. I resigned. That same morning, within the same hour of my resignation, I received a call from Pacific Gas and Electric Company of San Francisco.

"Have you accepted a position yet anywhere in the Bay Area?" the recruiter asked. I said no. The recruiter asked me for a recommendation, so I said, "You can talk to my boss right now. I just resigned." My supervisor, and (his boss) the department vice president, spoke to the recruiter, and gave me a favorable recommendation.

PG&E flew me out for an interview and made me an offer on the spot. They moved the entire family to California and gave me a moving allowance. God provided. California, here we come!

CHAPTER SIX

Picture-Perfect

We were living on Stacy Street in Oakland, California, just across the Bay Bridge. It was our fourth home in our ten-year stay in California. Dennis loved moving. He loved renovating and decorating and starting over. I enjoyed it too. I liked checking out our potential new neighborhood and always moving up—better home, better school system, better life.

Life was getting better and better. Dennis was finally

making money and I, too, was doing well financially in California.

We had our last child shortly after moving to California. Dennis was happy stopping with two, but I wanted to try a third time for a daughter. I thought I had a good chance since my sister Mary's third child was a daughter. Dennis's father made me so mad when he found out I was pregnant.

"You're having another boy, you know," he said.

It wasn't a question but a statement of fact. I ignored him and was still hopeful, especially when people would say things like, "You're carrying low, you're definitely having a girl."

But Dennis's father was right. Boys ran in their family. All boys!

My pregnancy with Eddie was uncomfortable; he kicked *all* the time. Just as with his brothers, I was scheduled for a C-section. But medical science had advanced and the anesthesia kept me from pain until they got me up to move me around after the birth. This was the first time I experienced a pain-free birth. Dennis was in the room with me the whole time. He even got to see the doctors tie my tubes, sealing that this would indeed be our last child.

We were both very happy about that. But we were even happier to see our third son in the flesh. When he came out, it seemed as if his whole body was covered with hair. When the doctor announced that it was a boy, we both forgot about wanting a girl. We didn't have a name picked out, though. We hadn't talked about it at all during the pregnancy. I asked Dennis about a name when he came to the hospital the next day and he said, "Eddie."

"What?!"

"His name is Eddie," he said quietly.

Dennis's father was named Eddie. Despite his fear of his father, Dennis loved and cherished his dad. He always remembered the one tender moment they had shared when Dennis decided to leave Ohio for Alabama to take a new job. His dad said in that intense, deep voice, "Son, if you don't make it, you can always come home."

So Eddie Andrew Meredith it was. He came into the world much like his grandfather—kicking and screaming. He was a complete handful from the very beginning. But it was love at first sight.

Our family was complete and the church was thriving too. It was growing by leaps and bounds. Dennis was singing and preaching better than he ever had. I officially joined the church so that I would have a vote at annual meetings. I also joined the choir and worked in the Sunday school department, teaching the teens. This was all the involvement I thought I could muster while working full-time at PG&E, being a mom of three young boys, and being a good wife. I still managed to find time to do one more thing, however—I expanded our children's ministry at Mount Calvary Missionary Baptist Church (MBC), going to the community outside of the walls to build it, wearing out our blue van picking up kids. We formed a children's choir that became so popular they were invited to sing all over the city.

MBC's deep affiliation with the National Baptist Convention (NBC), the California State Convention (state delegation of NBC), and the district associations expanded Dennis's preaching arena. One Sunday, a guest preacher came to speak at MBC to raise money for a missionary campaign in Africa.

That Sunday was magical.

The church was packed. After the choir sang a soul-stirring rendition of "We'll Understand It Better By and By," Dennis joined in with his deep bass voice and upstaged them all, singing it slow with deep emotion. Then he picked up the pace and whipped the entire church into a frenzy.

By and by when the morning comes,
All the saints of God are gathered home,
We'll tell the story how we've overcome:
For we'll understand it better by and by.

When Dennis was finished, women were throwing purses at him, falling out, shouting. It was pandemonium and the spirit was high. (Dennis later made a CD, produced by my son Taylor, featuring this rendition of the song. It was his late grandmother's favorite hymn.)

The guest preacher, Reverend Wallace, a slender, light-skinned man, came to the podium to deliver the sermon.

"The National Baptist Convention's mission in Africa needs you . . ." he started, directing his comments to Dennis.

Reverend Wallace was a powerful preacher, and as he explained the deplorable conditions in Africa in detail—talking about famine and lack of clean water, sanitary conditions and disease, people wept. Dennis made up his mind to go. He wanted to be a part of this African missionary trip.

I didn't like the idea because we had just had Eddie. Eddie would cry and cry and cry, for no reason, and nothing seemed to pacify him except his father. He was strictly a daddy's boy, and he would only take breast milk for three months. But Dennis went to Africa anyway. His mom came and helped me while he was gone.

When he got back twenty-eight days later, his back was messed up from riding over the rough terrain, as he went from village to village, preaching. It was there that he met a man who would become his best friend. Dennis couldn't stop talking about Franklin.

He also talked about how people had traveled far just to hear him, how they ran to church for the services. And also how appreciative they were. He told us about the interpreter who translated the services. His explanation was so descriptive that we felt as if we were right there. I wished I had been there with him. He came back full of enthusiasm about his ministry.

The next Sunday, we had Eddie's baby dedication service at MBC. Dennis had brought back an awesome black knit dress from Africa for me to wear at the ceremony.

By the time we moved to Stacy Street, Eddie was five. The house and the neighborhood were handpicked by my beloved husband. It was a tree-lined street of beautiful homes, with great schools and lots of children in the neighborhood.

Every house on the block looked like the next. It was very homogenous, but Dennis was determined to make ours stand out—at least on the inside. He had all of the bathrooms remodeled, and the kitchen, too. He took down a wall, opening the kitchen area into an enlarged family room. We added a deck in the backyard with fruit trees and flowers. And we pulled up all of the carpet to reveal the beautiful hardwood floors.

Dennis made it beautiful, the way he had made every home we lived in. We were such a happy family. People at the church or anyone who observed us together would call us "the Huxtables." We were very demonstrative—always laughing and sharing affection.

The boys were the center of our universe. I was the PTA president and made sure the boys got good grades in school. We tucked them in at night. I always read them bedtime stories so they would love bedtime.

"Come on, Mom, we have the reading house ready!"

They would create a tent by draping sheets from the top of

the bunk bed to create their "reading house." I would come into the tent and totally captivate them by acting out the roles of each character in the book. I would read to them until they got sleepy. This was a nightly ritual, and the boys and I loved it. It was such a special time for me with my sons.

I coached Taylor to victory in a citywide oratorical contest three years in a row. He won the first time in the fourth grade, reciting Dr. Martin Luther King Jr.'s, "I Have a Dream" speech from memory. My job was to teach him to over-pronounce his words—say the endings of every word, articulate, and be expressive. Taylor was (and still is) a natural, with presence, with voice, and a memory like an elephant—total recall. Like father, like son.

Dennis would cook breakfast each morning—usually oatmeal and fruit—and made sure the kids got off to school on time. Because I worked long weekday hours, Dennis would have a multicourse dinner on the table every night, which included a meat, two vegetables, bread, and the best sweet tea in the world. We ate family style daily, and dinner was a very sacred time for our family. This was when the boys would share their daytime experiences. Micah would tell on Taylor for getting in trouble at school for being talkative, and Taylor would tell on Micah for "acting like a girl." (More on this later.)

Every weekend we would plan something different to do as a family. But first, I would get up and cook a down-home breakfast—fried fish and grits, homemade pancakes and peach compote, the works! (My daddy would have been proud.) Every Saturday we would be out of the house for the day—riding bikes in the park, skating, or swimming at the YMCA. Twice a year we would take family vacations to places like Disneyland and the nation's capital, and whatever church convention was scheduled for that year. The boys loved going to the Edwin Hawkins Music & Arts Seminar. Dennis was treasurer for the Music and Arts Seminar.

As I mentioned, Dennis planned most of our vacations. But I did plan one particularly memorable family vacation—a skiing trip. From where we lived, you could drive three hours and be in the mountains and ski.

I couldn't believe I could plan something the whole family would enjoy, because that was usually Dennis's forte. None of us had ever been skiing, so it was exciting doing something together for the first time. The drive through the narrow snowy roads was scary, though. But Dennis was at the wheel and I felt completely safe.

The boys were ages eleven, ten, and five. When we got there, we couldn't wait to hit the slopes. We all took one-hour ski lessons. The boys, including Eddie, were ready to go in one hour, zipping down the mountain as if they had skied their entire lives. I was in brake mode all the way down that mountain. Dennis stayed with me (even though he could handle more demanding terrain), and we had a ball.

When we finished, after a day of skiing, we all hopped into

the heated pool to relax. It felt like heaven. It was one of the most exhilarating vacations we had ever had. And I was the one who planned it. Dennis and the boys were thrilled. We had a ball.

I was so happy. I was with my best friend, with whom I'd ended up falling in love. Our children were perfect beyond my wildest imagination. And we had created this beautiful home and even more beautiful family.

I thanked God every day.

CHAPTER SEVEN

Fix It, Jesus!

I started to see some changes in Dennis after Eddie's birth. He seemed distracted, but I couldn't put my finger on it. It wasn't significant enough for me to make a big deal out of it. I thought for a minute that he resented the third birth. But I quickly ruled this out because he was such a devoted and caring father. And he loved the pieces out of Eddie.

The real difference wasn't in how he treated the boys or how he was in the family, but in how he treated me. I started to have dreams that he was having an affair and was leaving me. The wife of the organist in our church called me one night, out of the blue, and told me that Dennis was a hypocrite.

"What do you mean?"

She said, she saw one of Dennis's friends in downtown Oakland acting very flaming—as in very feminine.

"My husband is no hypocrite!" I said, and I didn't speak to her for a while after that.

Dennis came back from Africa with a new friend, who would end up being one of his best friends over the next twenty years. Franklin was also a pastor. The two began traveling around the country meeting up with other pastors of huge congregations. Dennis and these pastors would go on "retreats" and Baptist conferences/conventions frequently.

I wasn't keen on attending all these conventions. But every now and then, it would become a vacation for the boys, who were all talented musicians, singers, and orators. I thought it would be good to expose them to professionals in the gospel arena.

Micah was an awesome singer, and Taylor was a talented percussionist and orator. Eddie was an excellent orator and could pluck out tunes on the piano but wouldn't sit still long enough for lessons. From the time that Eddie was able to make a complete sentence, he would always say that he wanted to be a preacher, just like his daddy.

We had to move again because the landlord on Stacy Street wanted to move back into her house. Dennis found a house in

Redwood Heights that he fell in love with. The view was spectacular—we could see the city of San Francisco from our living room. Needless to say, we loved the house, but the owner did not want to sell. We lived there a couple of years after Eddie's birth; but soon Dennis started looking for another home for us and found one on the other end of Stacy Street. This house had four bedrooms and three baths and was bigger than the first house he'd wanted. The neighborhood was also more suitable for raising three active boys.

We renovated the whole place. When Dennis got through, it was a showplace. Even though we had four bedrooms, we bought a bed with a twin on top and a double on the bottom, and the boys shared the same room. They loved being together.

We enrolled Taylor and Micah at Grass Valley Elementary School. They had just begun searching for a new school principal, and I became a part of the selection committee. We selected an outstanding candidate, Mrs. Parker. I served as president of the PTA (under her superior leadership) until the boys finished school there. I personally knew all the teachers and all the administrators, and this was good for my children. They all got a great start there.

When it was time for Eddie to attend preschool, I put him in Horizon School, where Micah had gone when he was preschool age. After just two weeks, I got a call from work to come get Eddie. This was the beginning of the drama we would have with Eddie his entire school life. Eddie was expelled from preschool (at the age of two years old) because he was too aggressive. Whatever he wanted, he took; if anyone resisted, they would get hurt; and if anyone bothered him, they would get hurt. I said to Dennis, jesting, "I told you not to name my baby after your daddy!"

But we worked together as a family to keep Eddie in line, and he eventually excelled in school.

We kept the boys busy. I made sure they had plenty of opportunities to explore their interests. Taylor took drum lessons, Micah took singing lessons, and Eddie took piano lessons. We always kept a piano in the house. Everyone could play. I could only play from sheet music and not that well. Taylor started playing drums for the church and Micah was doing well; he would do solos at different churches in the area, and Micah was lead singer in the MBC Children's Choir.

Dennis and I were a team with the boys. I handled the academics and extracurricular activities and provided encouragement, fun, and discipline. Dennis would prepare breakfast for the boys and get them off to school in the morning, and have dinner ready when I returned home from work. We would all sit down to a hot family dinner at the end of each day and laugh and talk. Before bedtime, it was homework and reading time.

In my mind, Dennis and I had been happily married for thirteen years. I loved him and my family with all my heart. My sun rose and set on the assurance and the commitment of his love and the love of my children.

But one Saturday morning my whole perspective changed. It was the beginning of what would end up being the roller-coaster ride of my life—a horrible, rickety roller-coaster ride.

Sex the previous night had made both of us comatose the morning after. Dennis had sucked and kissed every inch of my body, from my head to my toes—literally. He sucked each toe and licked and massaged my feet. The hour I had taken preparing for bed had been well worth it. Dennis's penis entered me and filled me—driving me crazy—my Kegel muscles squeezed his penis as he moved in and out of my wet vagina. We exploded, coming together in our brass bed, with moans of gratification. Perfection!

The morning after: Dennis and the boys had gone to the store; and I was at home cleaning and washing clothes in the garage. While I was waiting for the drying cycle to complete, I was tidying a typically messy garage and stumbled upon a video. When Dennis returned from the store, the boys went outside to play, and Dennis walked into the kitchen.

I confronted him, "Dennis, what is this?!"

I repeated this statement several times, holding the video directly in Dennis's face. Dennis was stunned and at a loss for words; he was horrified that I had discovered his hiding place for adult videos.

Dennis replied, "How did you find this?" But I kept screaming.

After I calmed down, we began to discuss the video. Dennis

began to justify watching adult videos/pornography. His father kept adult/pornographic magazines in the bathroom, under his bed, hidden all over the house. Growing up exposed to porn, he thought nothing of this practice; his mother had knowledge of this practice with no objections—the material was hidden to keep it from Dennis and his brothers. I objected with righteous condemnation, questioning Dennis's morals and his calling. "Dennis, you are a preacher and a pastor!" My contention continued throughout the night until the wee hours of the morning, despite knowing Dennis had to preach the next morning. We went to church as usual; after church there was no discussion.

Monday morning, I rushed out of the house to catch my bus to the BART train to San Francisco to arrive at my job on the twenty-first floor of the PG&E building. Dennis called me at work and said, "When you get home, I will tell you everything."

My day went quickly—I was consumed with work the entire time. There was no time to think about the video. I had developed the art of mentally setting aside what I needed to set aside in order to function in the moment. I was practicing denial, suppression, and avoidance!

When I got home, the boys were not there. Dennis had gotten a babysitter and we had the entire house to ourselves. We chose the bedroom to talk. Dennis sat in the peachy orange armchair next to our brass bed. I undressed, put on my pajamas, and sat up in the bed. Dennis began to speak.

"Lydia, I am bisexual," he said. "I have sex with men. I

meet men in shopping malls, restaurants, grocery stores, and restrooms. Every encounter is sexual. Some nights, I go to 'The Jack-Off Club' in San Francisco."

He described the places, the type of men he was attracted to, and the sexual acts he would perform. He told me that the sex he had with men was low risk because it mostly consisted of men performing oral sex on him. He said he would never allow any man to penetrate him. He didn't like that.

"Baby, it's just sex," he said. "I love you and I want my family."

He said that he had never wanted an intimate relationship with a man because he'd had a terrible experience with a boy when he was a teenager, and he'd vowed he would never get involved in a serious relationship with another man. It hurt him so bad.

I just sat there, staring straight ahead. I was nearly in the fetal position when he was done, clutching my knees to my chest. I was numb, speechless, emotionally bleeding, wounded, and shocked. I imagined he could see my anguish all over me. I wear my emotions. Transparency is my virtue.

He broke the silence.

"There are others like me. When I went to Africa for the mission trip, I followed one of the ministers into the restroom and discovered he was just like me—married with children. His wife knows, and he told me I should tell you. His wife is fine with it. She even buys him condoms."

I was repulsed by this admission. I wanted no part of this "friend" or his stupid wife. I didn't want to share my husband sexually with *anyone*. I didn't want him taking off his clothes and exposing himself to anyone except me! I was livid.

I had never contemplated what bisexuality or homosexuality meant in terms of my faith until Dennis told me he had sex with men. I was not aware of the hatred that existed against gays/homosexuals/same-gender-loving folk until I was trying to get help and save my marriage.

Of course, the first place I turned to was the Christian community. And what I faced was more judgment, hostility, and hatred than I could ever imagine. That's when I learned that most Christians believed that homosexuality was a "sin against God" and that "God hates homosexuals."

Of course, I'd read my Bible and had even heard sermons preached from the Book of Romans listing sins that God "hates." But none of it resonated with me until I learned— thanks to my husband's admission—that I was married to a man who also had sex with men.

I just wanted to know how I could stay married to my husband, whom I loved, and keep my family together. I didn't care what these "Christian" folk said the Bible said—there had to be another explanation, another interpretation.

Dennis and I went to counseling. The first counselor said that Dennis would never change and that I either had to accept that or walk away from the marriage. We both cried that night in the parking lot after leaving his office, and when we got home in bed, in each other's arms.

I was listening to a Christian radio broadcast from the group Focus on the Family on my way to work. They were doing a show on homosexuality and treatment programs for homosexuals. I called Focus on the Family to get a referral for one of these programs. I told Dennis that if he refused to go, our marriage would be over. So he went.

Dennis hopped on his motorcycle on a nice sunny day, perfect for the ride. It was a five-hour drive to Los Angeles. The facility was called (through my foggy recollection) the Meier Clinics: Christian Counseling and Mental Healthcare. Dennis checked in. My insurance covered the entire cost of the treatment. They gave him a tour and escorted him to his living quarters, which he shared with another man. Later that evening, Dennis was in a group session with a therapist, and they began to discuss why they were there. Dennis told them he was there because he had sex with men and was married. He was told there that his issue was depression. They didn't try to discuss the possibility that Dennis might actually be gay because he had sex with men. The counselor never even used the words *gay* or *homosexual* or *bisexual*—as if the words themselves were abhorrent and demonic. For the entire week there were group sessions on how to come out of his state of depression. During his visit, Dennis saw a psychiatrist, who recommended that Dennis take drugs to reduce his sexual appetite. The drugs would help Dennis manage his desire for men. Dennis was afraid to take any medicines that would interfere with his sex drive. Dennis called me and explained the treatment plan and the drug prescription.

I told Dennis, "Come home immediately!"

I didn't want anything interfering with the quality of our sex life. So, Dennis checked out and came home. They gave him a list of therapists to select for follow-up treatment. Dennis and I sat together on the brass bed, seeking a therapist who appeared not to be a part of the Black church community for reasons of confidentiality; fate guided us to Dr. Jordan. Dr. Jordan was a black female, and she turned out to be an outstanding professional.

Dennis and I went to Dr. Jordan together. During our first visit we learned a new word: *dysfunctional*. We had never heard that word and its use with family dynamics. We both denied, vehemently, that our families were dysfunctional.

I stated, "My family is fine. Dennis's family is screwed up."

We both had a rude awakening, discovering that despite the religious tradition of my family, and the tight-knit intimacy of Dennis's family, both our families were "severely" dysfunctional—shaping our lives, infusing our lives with emotional and social issues that we would battle for the rest of our lives.

We had couple sessions and individual sessions. It was during our individual sessions that she took us way back into our past and guided us to our present. Her diagnosis of my condition was workaholism. Her diagnosis of Dennis's condition was sexual addiction.

After "detox" from the Focus on the Family–referred clinic, and during our counseling with Dr. Jordan (a Focus on the Family–recommended Christian counselor), we were directed to attend Exodus International for support group treatment. Exodus told Dennis that no one is born homosexual any more than a person is born an adulterer. He had to go through several sessions where they discussed his relationships with his father and other male figures and how these were the root of his feelings.

Dennis went through the Exodus program because I told him he had to do something to save our marriage. Exodus had weekly support group meetings similar to those held by Alcoholics Anonymous.

Exodus insisted that Dennis's desire for men needed to be broken—because "same-sex" sex was sinful. According to many observers, groups like Exodus (which in 2013 shut down its "gay cure" ministry and apologized to the gay community) and Focus on the Family fueled such hate and discrimination that are responsible for violent crimes and shameful acts against these groups of Americans, which have resulted in suicide, sickness in every domain (physical, emotional, social, etc.), rape, prostitution, homelessness, even murder! According to noted journalists, Focus on the Family and cohorts have spent billions of dollars pushing the agenda internationally that God hates gays, same-sex marriage is against God, and people who live in same-sex partnerships are condemned to hell. The counselor told Dennis that he wasn't fit for the pulpit.

This kind of propaganda made me sad (and still makes me sad today). It reminds me of the Southern Baptist apology coming hundreds of years late, after millions of people of color drowned in the Atlantic Ocean rather than endure the reality of chattel slavery (dehumanizing acts); and millions killed because of the abhorrent conditions of slavery and slave ships (where men, women, and children were packed together like rats without proper ventilation and no other place to release bodily fluids, vomit, and feces, except on each other). Lord, have mercy.

Dennis and I, playing "eeny, meeny, miny, moe," hand-picked Dr. Jordan from the referral sheet given to Dennis after he left "detox." My diagnosis and treatment plan by Dr. Jordan was a little different. Dr. Jordan told me that I was a workaholic, which I denied. But she gave me homework to do.

"Lydia, I want you to take this diagram and place on it the amount of time you spend doing everything that you do, and the amount of energy you use to do everything that you do, and bring this back to our next session," she told me.

I couldn't wait to prove her wrong. Being the engineer that

I was, I started out with that pie chart with precision, counting every hour I spent at work, every hour I spent as PTA president, every hour I spent working at the church, etc. Then I overlaid that pie chart with the amount of energy I expended at work and doing other things and how much energy I had left for my family.

I was ashamed to discover that I had so little energy left for my family, which I claimed to put first, which I claimed to love more than life. On a typical weekday, I expended fourteen to fifteen hours working, two to three hours with my family, and eight, sometimes six hours sleeping.

When I returned to my session the next week, I had my head hung down.

"Well, what did you find?" she asked.

I said simply, "You were right."

The family evaluations, the books she assigned us to read, and the prescribed activities she gave us "appeared" to help. They forced Dennis and I to be more attentive to each other, more accountable to each other, and more observant of our behaviors. We simply had to make time for each other.

Finding babysitters was easy. Dennis was pastor of a church with now more than seven hundred members. Everybody wanted to babysit our children. The boys had no clue we were going through this drama. Maybe they did, but they didn't understand. They were still quite young—all still in elementary school.

I remember the following Saturday after Dennis told me about his double life. I sent the boys to the neighborhood golfing range.

"What's wrong, Mama?" Taylor said, sensing something was amiss.

"Nothing, baby," I said. "Mama has a headache. You all run along now. And keep a good eye on your brothers."

I called my mother but I didn't tell her any details. I simply asked her, "Mother, did Daddy ever cheat on you?"

She said, "Yes!"

"What did you do?"

"I started my own bank account," she said. And that was all she said.

Prescribed activities that we enjoyed were the weekly date nights and readings from various authors about our addictions (his to sex, mine to work). Self-examination was a hard pill to swallow.

I remember a session we had where she asked Dennis, "Why do you suppose you seek out sex with men?"

Dennis said, to my surprise, "Lydia doesn't want to have sex enough."

"Well, how many times do you want to have sex a week?" she asked.

Dennis quickly responded, "About five times."

The therapist restricted us to sleep in separate bedrooms for a month. I couldn't believe what happened. Every other night either Dennis was sneaking into my room or I was sneaking into his room for sex.

Whatever happens in Dennis's personal life ends up in the pulpit. I feel that the therapist telling him that he was unfit to serve as pastor struck a chord, too. We were both assigned the book *Secrets of the Family Tree* to read. Dennis preached several series out of this book during our therapy.

Psychotherapy was now a part of our lives. We went every week, and every week we experienced a new awakening, learning something we didn't know about ourselves or our relationship, something that helped us get through another week together as we faced the most challenging issue in our lives. We followed our prescribed activities because we loved each other and we loved our children more than we loved our addictions and we wanted our marriage to work and our family to stay together. During this time, we both wanted the same thing.

Dennis stopped traveling with his friends. He told them about the therapy, but his words fell on deaf ears. He cut them off. We decided to make it. We decided to make it work.

Therapy continued for two and a half years. We were refocused on our marriage and our family.

During our therapy, Dennis and I both celebrated our fortieth birthdays. He surprised me by flying my mother and my oldest sister, Tricia, to my surprise birthday party. Things were going well and we seemed to be getting back to normal.

He rented a room in a fancy hotel on the waterfront. We had a wonderful weekend. We checked out on Sunday and went to church. When I got there, my mother and Tricia were sitting in the front pew. I screamed with joy. When we got home, Dennis had the house decorated, food catered, and friends were everywhere. I was so surprised and happy I couldn't eat anything. He outdid himself.

I couldn't let him outdo me, so the next year for his birthday I bought him a black motorcycle, and planned a surprise seven-day cruise. In the early years, I would buy Dennis gifts for different major occasions like Christmas and birthdays, but he never liked my taste. So I took him to pick out his own bike. And we left on the cruise the day after the party I threw for him.

The cruise was wonderful and he couldn't wait to get back to ride his new motorcycle. We were in a good place during this time. There was no more talk about bisexuality, homosexuality, jack-off clubs, or porno movies.

We learned to read each other. When he was anxious, I would pull him back. And when I was off balance with work, Dennis would remind me to get back to the center.

I was doing very well at PG&E. They were in the process of downsizing and informed me that I was in line to become their new assistant to the senior vice president. I was moving up the corporate ladder and making even more money. I was pleased with my progress, but I really wanted to start my own business.

Things were going well, but we needed a change of scenery. It was time to head back home.

I think the therapy was great for us, but it was also emotionally exhausting. Our therapy ended when our therapist moved to another state. We didn't want to start back up with someone new.

One date night, I shared with Dennis, "Baby, the company is downsizing and giving out these great packages—a year's salary. That's $100,000 to use to build a business."

"I think it's time to go home, Lydia," he said.

I called my mother, because this would mean giving up a career move that would position me to be in senior management. I had worked my entire corporate life to get to this place. So I needed to consult with someone who I thought would give me the best advice.

Mother simply said, "Follow your husband."

Dennis began his search for vacant churches in the South. We had prepared and sent out three résumés. Dennis ended up being a finalist for the head pastor position at a church in Nashville.

The strangest thing happened then. By a miracle, we'd gotten to California without spending a dime out of pocket. And the same thing would happen coming home.

Charles Ayers, a musician who had been homeless and who had stayed with us awhile when we were in California several years before, heard we were moving back South. He was now doing well and had some connections in Atlanta. Charles was in a position to help us find a new church home. Charles called our home in California while Dennis and I were on vacation in New York City for the National Baptist Convention. There would be no more conventions without Lydia Meredith attending. We were not at home when Charles called, but our good friend Shari happened to be at the house, checking the mail, when the phone rang.

She took the message and called us at the hotel to relay Charles's request, which was, "Why don't you guys fly to Atlanta and let me show you around to some churches that need a pastor?"

So we did. Charles picked us up from the airport that Saturday and showed us around the city, taking us to three vacant churches. The third church was Tabernacle Baptist Church (TBC), and the pulpit chairman was walking out of the building when we drove up. Charles knew him and began to chat, introducing us to the man, Mr. Mitchell. He invited us to come worship the next day. So we did.

I was sharp as a tack, from head to toe, as was Dennis. Mr. Mitchell saw him in the audience and called him up for a few words and a song. Dennis slayed them. He had the congregants hollering, shouting, dancing, clapping; the Spirit moved in the hearts of the members. After the Tabernacle service, we went to find Charles, who had to play at another service nearby. We thanked him for the lead. We even saw a young man we had taught in Sunday school at Sardis at that service. What a coincidence!

On Monday, Charles picked us up from the hotel and drove us to the airport to fly back to California. Monday night, we got a call from the pulpit committee, requesting that Dennis return to preach and interview for the position of pastor. We got a second call that night. In a matter of minutes, we went from elation to sadness. The second caller told us that our angel/tour guide, Charles, had just died of a massive heart attack.

Dennis and I gazed at each other in amazement. "Oh my God!!!"

A week later, Dennis got another call from the Nashville church where he was a finalist to come preach and interview with the pulpit committee. I heard Dennis say on the phone, "I'm sorry, I have accepted a position already."

I ran into the room afterward and said, "Dennis, are you crazy? They haven't hired you to pastor that church yet!"

Dennis responded, "Lydia, we are going to Atlanta. Where's your faith?"

I still didn't have a job. I figured I would start my search when we got there and settled. I put in a call to Southern Company, from which I had resigned before moving to California.

My old boss there assured me that I could return; however, when he told me that the workload would be grueling—eighty-plus hours a week was the norm—I decided not to go back. I was still in recovery from workaholism. Working there would take me back to ground zero.

When my package came through with a year's salary from PG&E, Dennis resigned from MBC. He gave them plenty of time to find a replacement, offering to stick around until a replacement was found. He wanted the transition to be smooth and not traumatic for the church. They refused to allow him to help in the transition or lend his expertise to select a worthy candidate. So we left sooner than we expected.

In the spring of 1994, all things were put in motion for our move to Atlanta. We were both without jobs, but we were moving to Atlanta anyway. His attitude was that if we had to start a church from scratch, we would.

It seemed as though everything was finally happening the way it was supposed to. We began our journey to Atlanta in a white Dodge Caravan, with three school-age boys and our dog, Pepper.

While traveling across country, we stopped to dine in Memphis. Mr. Mitchell, chairman of the TBC pulpit committee, called Dennis.

"Reverend Meredith, you are our new pastor!" he said

Once again, I was blinded by my own optimism and hope.

CHAPTER EIGHT

Sowing the Seeds

I realized through therapy that a lot of the things I allowed to happen to me in my life can be traced back to my childhood and upbringing. Isn't that the way it is for most of us? We are usually a product of our households. We either repeat the patterns or we fight like hell to do just the opposite.

I thought I was in the latter group, but discovered that like my mother, I was the kind of woman to stay in a bad situation, stick it out for the sake of the family, and ignore the things I wanted. I realized that the woman who raised me—who I thought was so mean sometimes and out of touch with us kids, who I thought I was nothing like—actually was very much a part of who I was to become as a woman. She was merely a product of her own upbringing and era.

My mother is a complex woman who I didn't understand for a very long time. She is a beautiful, dark-skinned woman, standing 5 feet 7 inches. She had long, beautiful black hair (now white and silky). On her next birthday, my mother will be ninety years young. I mean young too—she's vibrant and active. Her beautiful features and vibrant personality were not redeeming attributes in a world that measured your worth by the color of your skin. When she was growing up (and even when I was growing up) "dark skin" had a stigma. Dark-skinned people were treated poorly. For my mother, add to that child abuse and neglect. Both affected her.

My mother was born in poverty, the youngest of more than twelve brothers and sisters, and pregnant and homeless at age fifteen. Papa Leonard was a "weekend and holiday" alcoholic and very abusive to Big Mother. Big Mother was a spiritual, godly woman—she taught my mother to pray. Weekends and holidays were dangerous times for a young child growing up in the Leonard household—my mother used to hide under the house with Cheetah (her dog) to escape the commotion. The Leonards were not considered high society, so when my mother got pregnant at fifteen by Horace (high society), he chose the high-society girl to marry— who also happened to be pregnant at the same time as my mother—breaking her heart. She had so much shame and did not want to embarrass Big Mother (who had so much hope for her future) that she ran away, her mind set on having her baby and standing on her own two feet. Some folks would say, "Nothing good could ever come out of the Leonard household," but my mother would prove them wrong! But some of her siblings ended up being alcoholics and weekend brawlers like Papa Leonard.

My mother hopped on a bus headed out of town to look for an aunt whom Big Mother would often talk about. When she arrived in a town that is now called Cordell, Georgia, she just sat on a bench, not knowing where to start to look for her aunt. Mrs. James came by and saw her looking lost and despondent. She asked my mother, "Where are you going?"

Mother replied, "To my aunt's house, but I don't know where she lives."

Mrs. James answered, "Well, why don't you just come home with me, and live with me?" Mr. and Mrs. James rescued my mother from that bench, and took care of her until my oldest sister Tricia was born, up to eighteen months (just walking and potty trained). My mother worked the entire pregnancy and would give Mr. and Mrs. James most of her paycheck, saving the rest to provide for herself and Tricia, and for her journey back home someday.

My mother returned home with her toddler and Big Mother

immediately fell in love with Tricia. Shortly after, my mother left Tricia with Big Mother and journeyed to the big city—Macon, Georgia—to look for work. She ended up working at the same restaurant as my father (Wilbur Mitcham). My parents fell in love and got married (a love and marriage that lasted more than sixty years). Tricia joined my mother and father in Macon to set up household—Tricia was nearly five years old and was made to believe Daddy was her biological father. Daddy changed her birth certificate to Mitcham, adopting my oldest sister.

My daddy was light-skinned, but like my mother was born in poverty and was the youngest son of ten brothers and sisters. He was homeless at age seven. Both his parents died, and his grandmother, a full-blooded Indian, had also transitioned. They scattered. My daddy slept in vacant houses and under the bridge in Macon, Georgia. A family found my daddy under the bridge and took him in until he was old enough to go to the service. He received an honorable discharge from the army. He traveled to New York City and studied under some great chefs to become a cook. He returned to Macon and was hired as a cook at Len Berg's Restaurant, eventually working his way up to senior chef. He worked at Len Berg's all his life—for more than sixty years.

My parents had ten children together, and among us, some were light, some were dark, some had straight hair like mother, some nappy hair like Daddy. I got the nappy hair and in-between skin, a caramel color.

When I grew up, I stayed outside a lot, so I was perpetually darker than I actually was. And on top of that, I was skinny—not thin, but skinny.

One of my older sisters, Mina, was light-skinned with straight hair, and I felt that my mother treated her differently than the rest of us. My parents were a product of how they were socialized. I don't believe it was intentional, but I felt Mina was favored.

It wasn't that Mina got anything more than the rest of us. We were too poor for anyone to get much of anything. It was just the connection she had to Mother. To this day, Mina leads all of my brothers and sisters in making sure Mother is taken care of—from making sure the house is painted to making sure Mother has enough food. Mina's not the oldest, but she leads the family as it relates to our Mother.

Growing up in those times, just a couple of generations away from slavery, all of the self-hatred and pain and shame around skin color and "blackness" still weighed on us. No one talked about it. And there certainly wasn't any therapy being had back then. People just repeated patterns and carried on traditions—engaging in some of the same brutality that black folks suffered during the days of bondage, like beatings.

You would think giving birth to ten children would spark some motherly instincts. It didn't. Mother ran our house as if she were a drill sergeant in the military. The older siblings looked after the younger siblings while she and Daddy worked.

We each had chores and directives, and we had better do them well, or else.

My mother believed in "not" sparing the rod. She had a belt called "the police strap." It hung on a hook at the front door. You had to do something to warrant a beating, but once she got started, it was hard for her to stop. She beat my older brother once nearly half to death. I would pray that Lloyd would hurry up and cry so she would stop.

If one of us sassed her and she wasn't near the police strap, she would throw anything she could get her hands on. She threw a pot one time and hit my oldest sister, Patricia, in the head. Tricia, as we called her, was always saying things that mother felt were disrespectful. Tricia felt like she was just as "grown-up" as mother. She had so many responsibilities—she would take care of the younger siblings, cook, do our hair, do our laundry, and keep the house clean.

My parents hid from us that Tricia wasn't Daddy's child because it was taboo to have a child out of wedlock. But I knew she was treated like a stepchild. And that hurt me so bad. We were all disciplined and whipped. But Tricia's punishments just seemed so much harsher. My father never hit Tricia, but his words were so cold.

Tricia didn't care whether she got beat or not. She was going to say just what she thought. She told my mother once, "You don't need to be worrying about what I'm doing; you need to be worrying about what your own husband is doing!"

She would say things like, "Why do you keep having all of these kids? Why don't you get some birth control?"

Of course, she got beat for saying all of that. I would say to myself, *Tricia, why don't you just be quiet? Why don't you just hush?!* But she wouldn't. She got beat if she came in two seconds after curfew. My mother's rules were strict. I came home for Christmas break during my first year in college. I came in two minutes after midnight after hanging with my friends. My mother went off and embarrassed me in front of my friends. I finished my engineering degree in three years because I never went home for a break again.

I didn't understand when I was little why my parents treated Tricia so harshly. She was beautiful. She even won a beauty contest. Most of Tricia's beatings came because of boys. I guess it scared mother that Tricia might end up pregnant the same way she did. But Tricia was tough, not easily wooed, and worked hard and knew what she wanted for her future, and being a teen mother wasn't a part of her plans.

While Tricia seemed to constantly run headlong into my mother or father's wrath, I did everything in my power *not* to get a whooping. The only time Mother slapped me was when I was eleven. We were in the kitchen and I was helping her prepare dinner. I was washing the pots and pans that she had just finished cooking in and preparing the dishes to go onto the table. Mother didn't cook often because she was always tired after working all day.

On those rare days when Mother didn't have to work in other peoples' homes, she would wash our clothes and have dinner ready when we got home from school. Boy, I loved those days when we came home to a clean house and a hot meal from her.

I was in the kitchen with her—it was just the two of us—and I wanted to make a connection with her so badly. As I was drying a pot I asked, "Do you love me?" She looked at me and slapped me with the back of her hand so hard I saw stars. I guess this was an insult to her, or she was having a bad day, but what I needed that moment was simply to hear my mother say "Of course, I love you" because I had never heard those words from her before.

I remember another time while we were cleaning up after dinner. (We had to always clean up after we ate. My mother wanted everything washed and put away immediately.) I was pouring grease into a bowl from the frying pan where she had fried the chicken. Back then you saved the grease to use for another frying. In most homes, there would be a container of old grease on the counter.

As I was pouring this hot grease, some of it spilled on my hand. I started hollering from the pain. My mother didn't even look at it. I called my daddy, who was still at work. He left his job and took me to the emergency room. I had second-degree burns. I told the doctor, "Please don't let my hand looked crumbled up." I had a cousin who had a bad burn on his arm and face, and it was all crumbled and messed up. But thankfully, mine healed perfectly—with not even a scar.

My mother just wasn't the doting type. If you were sick, you had better get better. You didn't get any babying from her.

I figured out how not to get beatings—don't get caught—and to succeed in the classroom. Among her many rules, Mother demanded that we excel in school. If you brought home bad grades, she got the police strap. She wasn't hearing any excuses. But if you performed well, she would recognize you, pay you a *little* attention. You had to earn her attention. For me, growing up, I felt I had to earn her love.

My therapist (while being treated for "workaholism") said I was addicted to work because receiving love and attention in my household was based on performance. If I stood out, I felt love from my mother. So I overachieved in everything. My not-so-perfect childhood, which was strict, sheltered, and poverty-ridden, made me not just overachieve but also strive for perfection—even if I had to manufacture it.

Though we were poor, education was stressed in our home. Just the threat of a beating was enough to elicit good grades in academics and citizenship. I also went to excellent schools and had excellent teachers. I knew the preamble to the Constitution and the Gettysburg Address from memory when I was in the second grade. My teachers were just phenomenal. They stepped out of the classroom and had a real connection with us.

This was during segregation. Our education and our lives

were very important to our teachers. They were part of our community, and they felt even more responsible for our success because of the world they were preparing us for, where they knew it wasn't enough to just be good. They went above and beyond.

My sixth-grade teacher, Miss White, showed my mother by her example what it meant to be a good parent. (She encouraged my mother to finish high school and enroll in college.) It was Miss White who pressed my hair for the first time. I will never forget that. She doted on me and encouraged me. She told me I could do whatever I put my mind to.

Miss White wasn't the only one. All of our teachers were phenomenal, but so was our principal. She played "Ave Maria" every morning, and we had to recite the Lord's Prayer (this was before they banned prayer in school), and the Pledge of Allegiance. And every teacher had a belt in his or her drawer (this was before they banned corporal punishment in schools). Miss White didn't have to use it, though. We had no disciplinary problems in her classrooms. There was nothing but learning and the desire to learn there. Somehow, we all understood the importance of getting all we could out of our teachers. We were taught that education was our ticket out of poverty. Parenthetically, education was our family's ticket out of poverty: Tricia became a high school teacher, gifted by God to inspire poor teens to excellence. Cookie became a hospital laboratory supervisor and business owner. Lloyd became a mechanic and business owner. Mina started off teaching and then became a school principal. Mary started off teaching and became a business owner. Zack retired from the army and is studying at Harvard. Faye owns a school and a chain of hair salons in Florida. Charlotte is a corporate analyst and is completing a doctoral program. Julie, the baby of the family, recently completed her doctorate in education and is serving as a school principal in a school heavily populated with socially and economically challenged teens. And yours truly founded and manages Beacon of Hope, a twenty-year-old nonprofit corporation with a mission to strengthen families and communities, to ultimately lift poor children and their families out of poverty and transform distressed communities. The icing on this cake is my mother—completing college at the age of sixty-five—making front-page news in Macon, Georgia.

When I was fourteen years old, my school life drastically changed! It was the first time in my school life that I had experienced true humiliation. It was a moment that I would carry with me all of my days. When I think about it even now, tears begin to well up in my eyes.

Mother told me that I would be changing schools for my freshman year of high school. Nineteen other girls from our town and I had been selected to attend Lasseter High School on the other side of the tracks from where I lived in Macon, Georgia. It was an all-white, all-girls school. There were also twenty boys from our town who would be attending Mark Smith High School, the all-boys counterpart across campus.

It was 1966, and things were still boiling over racially in America, especially in the South. I spent my entire life until this time protected in our all-black environment. My dad was chef at Len Berg's; but still, both Mother and Daddy did domestic work in white people's homes. My brothers and sisters and I also went to work for white folks at an early age. We had dealings with white people, but always from afar, from that subordinate position. It was never from a place of equality. We understood that. We knew how to handle that.

My first day at Lasseter, I walked a mile to school. The principal, Ann Henry—I will never forget that name—called all twenty of the new black girls to the study hall for what was supposed to be orientation, or welcome to the school.

"I want you all to know that we don't expect much from you," she started. "In fact, we don't expect any of you to do well here. But you're here, and we will do our best to provide you with an education."

The heat started rising from the back of my head. I felt a lump rise in my throat. But I refused to cry. I felt worthless, really worthless. But I was also determined to prove Miss Henry wrong. I would succeed there.

After a tough day of hard stares and whispers and snickers

behind our backs, it was time to go home. A shiny school bus pulled up in front of the school and a bunch of the white girls got on. I figured I would get a ride home as well, since it was a long way back to my neck of the woods.

The bus driver looked at me as if I had lost my mind, but I ignored him and proceeded to find a seat. I sat next to this one girl toward the middle of the bus. She immediately got up and moved her seat. So I got up, too, and sat next to another girl, closer to the rear, as the bus was filling up quickly.

We had been sitting there for a while, waiting for the bus to pull off, when one of the girls said to the girl sitting next to me, "You ain't going to sit there next to that nigger, are you?"

It wasn't as much of a question as it was an accusation, which made that girl get up and move far away from me, as if I had some sort of disease or the cooties. I got up, too, and then got off the bus and walked home. I should have noticed that I was the only black girl on the bus. The other black girls must have gotten the memo about us not being welcomed on the bus.

When I got home, I told Mother what had happened that day.

"Don't even worry about that, Lydia," she said. "You're not a nigger or any of those things those girls called you. That's not who you are. You can do whatever you want to do, be whoever you want to be, if you work hard. You just make sure you work hard and show them."

My mother also gave me my marching orders: "You go back in that school with your head held high. And you don't treat them the way they treat you," Mother said. "You treat them the way you want to be treated."

I held on to that. Instead of withdrawing and being sad and angry all of the time, I ignored the insults (I was often called *monkey* and *blackie*), kept a smile on my face, and was friendly and jovial even to those who were nasty to me. I was so funny and outgoing that it almost became a game for me to see how many of these white folks I could turn around. Mother said, "You don't worry about fitting in. Just be you!" And it worked.

Thanks to the advice of my mother and the solid foundation I was given by my black teachers for most of my life, I had the confidence and skills to survive. For me, especially that first year, it was all about survival. Many of the nineteen girls who started with me didn't last past that first year. They couldn't take it. But I was determined not just to stay, but to be a standout.

In the tenth grade, I got tapped for the National Honor Society. My grades were high, and they had enough integrity to elect me to this prestigious honor. From that point on, people started talking to me. The teachers started talking to me differently when they found out that I wasn't stupid. If you look at my yearbook, I was first in everything. I was first-chair clarinet, in the band and the yearbook editor. I was even in the homecoming queen's court. I figured out if I could make people laugh it would be easier for them to like me. So I brought humor along with excellence into the classroom.

I understood that the only way to break down that barrier was to be excellent and exceptional and also be myself. I couldn't make them love me, but I could make them respect me. I tried out for the cheerleader squad my sophomore year. This was a big deal, because the school had never had a black cheerleader. I worked so hard and I knew all of the cheers. Everyone just knew that I would make the squad. But I didn't. They did, however, make me one of the alternates. Before the season started, one of the girls got pregnant and had to leave school. And guess what? I ended up on the team!

I went to games all over the county. And at every game, I was treated as if I had the plague. At first, even my own squad members treated me poorly. I missed our first practice because a couple of the girls lied to me and told me we didn't have practice. The physical education teacher, Miss Coleman, who also coached the cheerleaders, asked me why I'd missed practice. I told her what had happened. But she still sat me out a game for missing practice.

I understood there would be different rules for me. So my goal was to be better than every other girl. I was going to cheer louder, jump higher, and have more energy than all of them. And I was better than they were—far better. It was undeniable. Everyone knew it, and soon they had to accept it.

Be excellent. Be yourself. That was my formula for combating racism.

I took that formula into my work life. I knew I couldn't just work a forty-hour week. I knew I couldn't just sit at my desk and do the bare minimum. I needed to know everything about the company for which I worked. I read their annual reports. I needed to know how their business worked. I needed to know how I fit into their business plan. How my job fit into the scheme of things.

I knew I had to bring work home. And I knew I had to be the best. There was no getting around it. I became a full-fledged workaholic and I loved it.

My therapy revealed that my overachieving began in my childhood to earn my mother's love and attention. My therapy also helped me understand the complexity of my mother, and how she understood and defined love.

When we were very young, during our evening prayers, my mother would tell her girls, "If you want a husband like your father, you better start right now praying for God to send him." I was seven when I heard these words. My sun rose and set with my father, Wilbur Mitcham. Ergo, I did pray for just that. I just didn't know that my father might have been equally as complex as my mother, and what that prayer led to was a lot more than I'd bargained for.

CHAPTER NINE

Daddy's Girl

I grew up believing that my daddy was perfect. My mother painted this "perfect-picture" daddy for her children. He looked like Billy Dee Williams. He was charming and sweet. He was hardworking, present, and he loved us very much. He was God-fearing.

Mother told me that Daddy named me Lydia after the woman in Acts 16:14, the dealer of purple cloth from Thyatira, a worshipper of God. This woman and everyone in her household were baptized, and they invited Paul and the disciples to stay with her. "If you have judged me to be faithful to the Lord, come and stay at my home." After Paul and Silas are imprisoned and beaten, after they survive an earthquake that breaks open their prison doors, and after they convert and baptize those who were holding them captive, Paul and Silas return to Lydia's home before heading to Thessalonica to continue their mission.

My daddy had a vision for my life—Lydia, a woman of means, would be an active believer in God, would provide shelter for God's messengers.

Daddy worked as a chef, and he would get up early every morning because he had to prepare for the lunch crowd. He worked long, hard hours. He never took a vacation, and he was always home either in the mornings to get us off to school or in the afternoons before his night shift started at Len Berg's to give us—especially me—his attention. He wasn't like a lot of fathers I knew, who thought that as long as they brought home the money, they didn't have to participate in the lives of their children.

My daddy was there for me. He came to as many games as he could when I was cheerleading in high school, he came to my graduation from Vanderbilt, he gave me away at my wedding and he even came to see my husband installed as pastor at his first church. This was all a big deal for me because my daddy hated to travel, and, as I mentioned, he never missed work. So these were all stolen hours that he gave to me.

He would cook dinner for us every Sunday—his one evening off. My mouth waters to this day just thinking about my daddy's Sunday dinners. We'd sit down at the dining table as a family, enjoying the gifts of the best cook in the whole wide world. Some weekday mornings, we'd be treated to a full spread of fried fish and grits, eggs, bacon, and melt-in-your-mouth homemade biscuits.

And after our meal, my father would lead all of us in family devotion, where we would pray and give thanks for all of our blessings. I loved to hear my daddy pray. As he sat at the head of that table surrounded by all of his children and his wife, he would talk about how much he had to be grateful for. He would always begin his prayers by saying, "Dear God, here is your humble servant, bowing here before you, please hear my prayer, I am just a filthy rag in your sight, please don't let my sins fall on my children . . ." He would pray for what seemed like hours, but everyone stayed attentive until the end, when Daddy would say, "Let the words of my mouth, and the meditation of my heart, be acceptable in thy sight, my Lord, my strength, and my redeemer, Amen." Then he would add this phrase, as tears flowed down his cheeks: "We've done what God has commanded us to do, but yet there is room." These are precious memories.

He was a man who had a tough start in life, but he didn't let it beat him down. My father worked to provide for his family and he was there for all of us despite never having a role model for what a father should be—since he was homeless at the age of seven.

Daddy roamed about the small town of Macon, Georgia, living in vacant houses, before finally landing under the Ocmulgee River Bridge, where he found a homeless community. A couple found my father and took him into their home and raised him as their own until he was old enough to enlist in the U.S. Army.

My father was a proud and brilliant man. While he wasn't formally educated, he was an avid reader and practically memorized the *World Almanac*. Daddy would quiz us concerning state capitals, world capitals, and other facts from the *Almanac*. We had tons of books at the house, and each year, Daddy would buy the latest edition of the *World Almanac*.

My father was affectionate, warm, and compassionate. He greeted us with big hugs when he came home. I felt his love whenever I was in his presence.

Mother wasn't attentive to anyone's pain. My father used to complain about headaches. She didn't even offer to get him an aspirin. I later reasoned that she was in deep emotional pain herself and couldn't empathize with anybody else's pain at the time.

In contrast, my father looked like a saint. Because of this, I believe I had this rather unrealistic, and perhaps even naïve, view of the kind of man I needed to be with. If a guy didn't stack up to my father, I didn't have time for him. At the same time, because I discovered (at age fifty) that my father was less than perfect, I think I was more willing to see beyond flaws in the men in my life.

Still, perfect or not, I'm grateful for my daddy. He provided the balance for me in our home. When I went away to college, it was Daddy who made sure I was driven to my dorm. He bought me a record player. He wrote me letters those first months telling me how much he missed me. I still have one letter he wrote me after I made the dean's list at Vanderbilt. I framed it, because he called me "the sweetest one."

My daddy never lifted his hand to touch me in any kind of disciplinary way. I rarely even saw him angry. The only time I can remember him angry was when my sister Mary got burned when she fell on the heater. She was fine, but he held my mother responsible. That was the first time I even heard him raise his voice. He had a beautiful, melodic voice—yes, my daddy could sing.

He was the epitome of a man to me. I could call my daddy for anything. He was always there for me. And I was there for him.

My father confided in me when he was almost eighty years old, his health failing, that he was not the man I thought he was—not completely. He was definitely the father I needed and expected. But he wasn't the husband I thought he was. He confessed to me that he had families outside ours. He not only cheated on my mother, but he had other children. I had other siblings that I didn't know existed.

I remember vividly, as if it were yesterday. It was Thanksgiving—a typical Mitcham family reunion. The cars parked outside were a small example of the success we had all experienced—there were BMWs, Mercedes-Benzes, Cadillacs, Lincolns, all parked in front of my parents' home.

Daddy had cooked a meal to die for. Roast turkey, barbecue pork roast with his famous homemade barbecue sauce, collard greens, coleslaw, potato salad, cornbread dressing, creamed corn, yams, okra, tomato and cucumber salad, an array of cakes and pies, and his famous homemade peach icecream. My daddy would be so exhausted after working at Len Berg's catering and preparing this huge meal for us that he would retreat after dinner to his favorite rocker in my parents' bedroom. I pulled away from the entertaining banter of siblings, nieces, nephews, and friends to enjoy alone time with my Daddy. I was dressed as pretty as I could be because Daddy loved to see his eight girls all dolled up. He called us his little lambs and would tell each of us, on separate occasions, of course, "You're the sweetest one." I loved to hear him say it to me, even though I knew I shared this honor with all my sisters.

Finding Daddy, I flopped into his lap, my favorite place. He said, "Ly, you're the sweetest one." My oldest brother was on his way out as I entered, and my daddy yelled out his favorite phrase: "Smoking and drinking will strip the rags off your back!" Then he whispered to me in the same breath, "I never smoked and never drank, but I do have two or three outside children."

I looked at Daddy smiling, thinking he must be joking, or hoping that I hadn't heard what I thought I'd heard. Then he pulled out the names and addresses of these "outside" children, Lavern and Eric. Back in those days, you hid your indiscretions at all costs. My daddy was chairman of the deacon board in our church for as long as I can remember. And he was hiding this.

My father was the best-looking man in Macon, Georgia. I am sure he could have had just about any woman he wanted— and I later discovered he had his share. To my disappointment, he had unprotected sex on top of adulterous affairs. I was stunned. I was even more stunned when he said, "Ly, I want you to call your brother and your sister and introduce yourself."

"Daddy, are you sure?" I asked.

"Yes," he said.

I wondered why my daddy was telling me this secret he had hidden for more than twenty years. I am sure the stress of keeping this secret added to his illnesses, and the guilt caused him to punish himself, by not taking proper care of himself. Nonetheless, Daddy knew my love for him was unconditional, and obviously my mother's was too, because she must have suspected that he was cheating. But I wasn't sure if she knew about his outside kids.

About a week later, Daddy phoned me and asked me if I had called my brother and my sister. I told him no because I didn't know if Mother knew. He insisted that I call. So I called my oldest sister, Tricia, to ask her what I should do. Tricia was pissed that I would involve her at first, but as always she helped out her baby sister. While Daddy had adopted Tricia, she always called him Daddy. He was the only father she ever knew until she was nearly forty-five years old. Tricia called Daddy and Mother and put it all out, the way she always did. She called me back to let me know the path was clear.

I called my newly found brother and sister. My brother Eric was happy to establish a relationship with the family. My sister Lavern was not so receptive. Three weeks after that call, my father had a massive stroke. He slipped into a coma and never recovered.

For the funeral, I made sure that Eric and Lavern were notified. And my mother made sure that they also rode in the family limo. My mother took it all in stride. We never had a conversation about it, but she rolled with the punches. One of my mother's greatest traits I believe is her power to forgive. Even after finding out about these other children, she was there every day for my daddy through his stroke. She took care of my daddy as if he was a Barbie doll until he died. She also welcomed Eric and Lavern into our home and into our family (Lavern eventually came around). I finally realized how my mother suffered the years my father was unfaithful, and I had a different respect and admiration for her. And none of us ever knew about that struggle. We also never knew why she was often bad-tempered. Today, my mother's temperament is so different. She's warm, fuzzy, vibrant, fun, proud, and embraces me with love like my daddy used to do.

I was privileged to hear and execute my father's last request before he died. I knew he had a special kind of love just for me. In fact, I believed I actually was the sweetest one.

When I told Dennis about my father's outside children, he cracked up, broke out into uncontrollable laughter. The boomerang was too much to take. I had always made his father out to be the bad guy, because Big June's affairs were "open" and his mom (my mother-in-law) once told me that she didn't know if she would live to see her sons finish high school because of the physical battering she endured at Big June's hands. Mom had a sharp tongue and Big June had a fierce backhand. Dennis was petrified of his father, as were most.

While I had vilified and blamed Dennis's father for being a horrible example and role model for my husband, it turned out my father wasn't much better. What Dennis's father did in public, my father, in some respects, was doing in secret. He didn't beat my mother, but I'm sure his affairs must have broken her and made her feel battered.

I felt the sting of Dennis's laughter. I felt my father's fall made him feel justified for how he treated me all the years we were married. It made me angry not at men, or at my dad, but at Dennis. Learning about my father's affairs never changed how I felt about my father. Somehow I believed he had made recompense for his deeds, and my job was to love him only—and that I did without coercion. It was quite natural despite his known faults, maybe because our relationship had been cultivated before I found out.

What I learned was that my mother suffered, and I wondered how she managed to cover it up and endure, and what she gave up to give us a "healthy" view of our father. In the end, was this sacrifice really healthy for us emotionally? In some ways, it was. In others, it was not. She was doing the best she could under the circumstances to do what she thought was right.

Clearly, her actions did not help me pick a man who would not abuse me. It did not help me cope effectively with my abusive spouse. I cannot blame my mother for my demise, however. The societal pattern started way before my mother and father lived it out. We are victims of patterns. In my mother's generation, women stood by their men. They were expected to stay, keep the family together, no matter what. I couldn't help but continue the pattern.

There's something to be said for not throwing in the towel, not quitting. I know I was determined in that way with Dennis. I was willing to do whatever it took to keep us together.

The bottom line is that when a marriage fails, children suffer. We can speculate all day as to what's the best course. Studies show that children's brains are under construction until age twenty-five. Having a stable family in place for that long then becomes the ideal. However, if the family environment is filled with violence and unrest, it is reported that there is a negative effect.

For me, it was great having my daddy in the house. The illusion of perfection in my father, and the relationship he and I had, made me a strong, fearless woman. But I believe it also gave me a false sense of what to expect from men and my relationships.

It was great feeling my daddy was flawless, but it created intimacy issues with my mother growing up. And it cost my mother much more.

CHAPTER TEN

Reality Check

O nce we were Atlanta bound, I called the chamber of commerce and Department of Education to find out where the best schools were. Neither of us had jobs, and we couldn't afford private school. Having uprooted our boys, we had to make their well-being our No. 1 priority. This meant keeping our boys in environments in which they could cultivate their gifts and talents and stimulate their intellect.

After we decided on the Fayette County school district,

which boasted academic excellence and diversity—Dennis took a trip ahead of us to pick a house and a neighborhood. He chose the perfect house, as usual. It was unbelievable how big a house we could get in Georgia for $140,000. Each son had his own room, and we had a very nice master bedroom suite. Downstairs was the living area, with a sunken family room with a floor-to-ceiling fireplace. And there was a full basement that opened out to a terrace level. We signed the purchase agreement and made the down payment on the house before we moved.

My package from PG&E paid for the move and almost paid the entire mortgage on the house, so our cost of living was pretty low. This was important because I was not working, and Dennis's starting salary at Tabernacle was only $400 a week. We believed that being navigated to Tabernacle by our angel/tour guide was not coincidental. It was the hand of God.

The trip across the country was exhausting. Once we arrived, we stayed in the Red Roof Inn for a week until our furniture arrived.

I remember the faces of the boys when we moved into our 5,000-square-foot home, on discovering they each had their own room. They were all wide-eyed. Eddie was scared. He wasn't used to being by himself and he didn't like it.

We were all so excited, yet somewhat fearful of our new life in Georgia. Taylor didn't want to move because he had to leave behind so many friends. Being the new kid, especially going into middle school, is tough.

Micah and Eddie didn't care about leaving behind friends as much as leaving behind a familiar and beloved neighborhood. I was fearful because for the first time in my adult life I wasn't working. I felt out of control. *A housewife?* I had to find something to do. Quickly!

Dennis had to figure out the politics and the culture of his new flock. Every church has some baggage or dirty laundry that needs washing, and Tabernacle was no different. The church had split a couple of times. There had even been an alleged scandal involving the ex-pastor and some rumor of drugs and domestic violence. Little did they know that another type of addict and abuser was getting ready to take the reins.

Our first service was a shock for me. You could have thrown a football in this huge church and not hit a single person. I guess everyone who didn't want a new pastor had decided to stay home. This was the first Sunday in April, April 3, 1994. Dennis preached a sermon titled "Rolling Stones." Those who didn't show up missed a classic. Dennis was phenomenal that Sunday, and the next, and the next. It wasn't long before the few who were there spread the word. Dennis's preaching and singing filled those empty pews.

Tabernacle needed an office manager/secretary, and I needed something to do. I made $75 a week. I didn't care about the money. I would have done it for free. I was also volunteering at the boys' schools, even substitute teaching. And I started my own business—JCIL (Jesus Christ Is Lord) Software. The members were so nice to us and they were very happy with Dennis because he came right in making major renovations to the run-down church. He also engaged the surrounding community, which was plagued by drugs, homicides, theft, and blight. It was our kind of ministry.

I knew the pay would come. As my daddy always told me, "Church folks feed well." And while we weren't making much money, we never wanted for a good meal. One member and her husband, Brother Sam and Sister Willie Mae Evans, brought us groceries every other week.

We didn't find out until after Dennis's installation that the church was in such dire straits. There were three pending litigations, IRS threats on bank accounts, and someone had been stealing from the church's coffers. I had my administrative work cut out for me. Volunteering, housewife duties, and now this—I was back to my work-addicted self.

Soon, Dennis would be up to his old tricks as well.

It was a school day, and I was cooking breakfast as I did every morning before the bus came to pick the boys up for school. They finished a hearty breakfast and ran out the door when they heard the bus pull up in front of the house. Dennis helped me clear the dishes away, and then we retreated to the couch in the family room to cuddle and talk. This was our morning routine. It had been almost three years since our move from California, and we had settled into our new life quite nicely.

I was getting ready to go downstairs to do some work on the computer. We had set up a home office there for me to work in to avoid the twenty-minute drive to the church every day.

As I was heading downstairs, Dennis said out of the blue, "We're not going to make it, are we?" I stopped in my tracks and looked at him, confused.

"Why would you say that?" I walked over and gave him a strong, reassuring hug. But I didn't wait for an answer. I just trotted downstairs to begin my work. He followed me. He caught up to me and held me in his arms. After a long silence he confessed, "You need to get checked out for gonorrhea."

What?

I was livid. I pushed him away from me and didn't say another word. I left the house and drove straight to the doctor. I was crying the whole way. When I got to the doctor's office, I told the nurse through my tears that my husband had told me that he had gonorrhea and that I needed to be treated. I felt humiliated beyond words and so hurt. I also felt trapped. Trying to make this relationship work, I had turned down an engineering position at Southern Company and all the money and security that went with it. I no longer had the financial independence that came with working in corporate America.

We had moved from California. I had hoped that a change of scenery, counseling (which we had successfully completed), and being back closer to both our homes would finally put an end to the marital drama. It had seemed as though things were going well. The boys were growing up fast. Taylor was in his first year of high school, Micah was in middle school, and Eddie was in elementary school. Now here I was with this thing dumped in my lap. *Gonorrhea?* Why did I have to get checked out? I was supportive and faithful; I did not have sex outside the marriage.

Most women would have left after this. And believe me, I contemplated it. But I just wasn't willing to walk away. I actually believed the marriage could be saved, and it was ingrained in me that you didn't leave your family. You didn't take the easy route with a divorce. You endured. My mama endured. Big Mama (my grandmother) endured. I was going to endure.

Why didn't I just leave?

I have heard that question more times than I can say. I wanted to leave. My ego definitely wanted out. I was hurt, but I was emotionally connected to Dennis. He was the love of my life, the only man I felt completely myself with. We had three boys—all still in school. Was I just going to uproot them? Dennis may have been a philanderer and a liar, but he was the best father any child could imagine. Our priority was rearing our sons in a peaceful and lovely home. That became my purpose. And I was committed to the church too.

I wasn't prepared to leave.

We stayed in the same room, in the same bed. But for months, we didn't touch each other. He knew not to touch me.

Then one Sunday he preached this sermon, a powerful one—telling the church that I'd told him that I didn't like him anymore, and how he needed to fix that. He talked about how much he loved his boys and me. He told them how blessed he was to have us. It touched me deeply.

Dennis always had a way of preaching from the pulpit about our life. It was as if he could talk to me about his feelings better from the pulpit than in person. The pulpit was where Dennis's real power was. He used that pulpit to handle all of his problems. He would apologize from the pulpit in a way that was heartfelt and meaningful. Outside of the pulpit, Dennis was challenged to emotionally and socially confront personal issues and his lack of self-control.

I had hope. We went back to therapy. I thought this would fix it.

We had been in therapy for two and a half years in California after Dennis told me he was bisexual. We'd followed every instruction the therapist had given us (at least I had)—including her recommendation that we pray the gay away. Therapy had certainly made things better. I figured leaving that environment had opened the door for him to backslide. I knew therapy would help again.

We went to see Dr. Rosa McDaniel Ashe.

In our sessions, Dennis painted me as being a non-attentive, work-preoccupied wife. I told her that perhaps I worked so much to cover my pain and anxiety over what I knew about him. She gave us a book to read together—*The Dance of Anger* by Harriet Lerner.

In her book, Lerner posited that partners often do this dance of anger where one will do something to make the other one angry to get attention, and the partner will respond by escalating the angry situation. In order to heal, someone has to stop the dance—the anger. I knew we were doing this dance. Our dance was that the more Dennis would go out on his sexual escapades, the more I would work; and the more I would work (being distracted and absent) the less accountable Dennis would be. The dance made us enablers and codependent—our actions made it easier for our addictive natures to continue their self-destructive power in our lives. Dennis refused to read the book, but I filled him in on the details and started to put some of the advice into practice. I didn't engage in confrontation, nor did I approach him with accusations—even though I had plenty of reason to do so.

I am always looking for solutions, as if anything can be fixed. I love following a prescription, so I was grateful to have this book to read to help me better understand our issues.

Dr. Ashe gave us another assignment: Resume our Friday date nights. We had started those in California as part of our therapy there, and they seemed to make us more connected.

I never did tell Dr. Ashe the truth about why we were actually back in therapy—why *I* was there. I couldn't bring myself to tell her about the venereal disease Dennis drama, and I couldn't tell her the real truth—that Dennis was gay. I realize, looking back, that this lie made our sessions with her a waste of time and money.

After the STD drama, Dennis's behavior was becoming more out of control, and our marriage was unraveling quickly. He wasn't taking the therapy seriously. Instead, he found a nice distraction to take me away from our troubled marriage—blueprints for a new home he wanted to build for us. We would go over plan after plan during our date nights. We began driving through neighborhoods, getting ideas for construction. Then, finally, we decided on a house plan and sought out a builder.

We selected John Hightower, a renowned homebuilder in Fayette County. He began searching for a lot for our home. He picked us up one evening and took us to this plot of land. It was so beautiful, and fronted on a lake. The new home would go here. We became consumed with building our dream home. Putting our marital problems on the back burner was an emotional relief.

We built our dream home from the ground up. It took less than a year. We had every amenity I could possibly imagine. It was 8,000 square feet, with a pool in the backyard. We even had a lake a hundred feet beyond the pool, teeming with fish. When family would visit, they would fight through the wooded areas, the snakes, and the insects to get out there and fish.

I could just sit outside in the back and it was like being on a retreat. It was so peaceful, so beautiful, and so serene. The house was like something you'd see in one of those architecture design magazines. Dennis's taste was eclectic and very creative. The house was a showplace. Every space was furnished. He would have it no other way.

The kitchen was an open concept with black-and-white tiles that shone like new money. It had a huge island with granite countertops. We had all stainless-steel appliances, complete with a double oven, which I needed for holiday cooking. There was even a little office space in the kitchen area with a desk where I kept my cookbooks. Cooking was an art and a science for me.

The dining room and living room were on the other side of the kitchen, which featured a beautiful fireplace and a floor-to-ceiling window wall through which the breathtaking landscape could be seen: you could just sit and sit and sit and experience God's presence. We had no blinds or window treatments, nothing to take away from the natural beauty of the woods that were our backyard.

A gathering room opened into the kitchen and provided entrance to a wooden deck for outdoor dining. The breakfast seating area was inside a magnificent bay window. The boys loved to bring their friends over for dinner after school just to show off the house. They loved our house. We all loved that house.

There were hardwood floors throughout except for the kitchens and bathrooms, which were tiled. Our master suite was to die for—a garden Jacuzzi tub occupied a bathroom corner and windows surrounded the tub; the tub also served as a divider separating Dennis's sink from mine. There was a walk-in closet the size of another bedroom, a walk-in shower, a stacked washer and dryer in the master bath area, and a reading room that had a big window through which you could see the curvy driveway and landscaped lawn that led into our small palace we called home.

There was also a full basement, which I insisted on because of storms in our area. But the basement also became a haven, a place for our huge families to stay when they visited. It was also a great entertainment retreat, with an exercise room, three bedrooms, a living room, a dining room, its own kitchen, a study for Dennis, and an office for me.

The boys were quickly heading to adulthood. They had their own space upstairs, which was accessed by a spiral staircase, for them to hang out with each other and friends to play video games or board games, or do whatever they wanted to do.

When we moved into this house, Taylor was finishing high school, Micah had one year left, and Eddie was graduating from middle school. Dennis's entire family traveled down for Taylor's graduation and stayed comfortably at the new house.

Holidays in this house were beyond memorable. It would often take me an entire week to shop and prepare for the dinner and decorations that would be displayed for Christmas. We always went to Macon for the Mitcham family reunion and traveled there during Thanksgiving.

Dennis loved the holiday season. He would shop for days, making sure the huge tree had so many gifts under it that it spilled way beyond the tree's boundary.

I had grown up dreaming about living in a house just like this one. As a child we used to sing songs and chants as we plucked the petals off a flower. And wherever you landed when the last petal was plucked would be your fate. We had a chant that went like this: "Brick house, wood house, raggedy ol' shack," and if you landed on *raggedy ol' shack* when the last petal of a flower was plucked, that would be your fate. I would pray to end my chant on *brick house*. The house we lived in growing up was a raggedy ol' shack on the red clay dirt streets of East Macon, Georgia, and it was the best a maid and a cook could afford, earning $35 a week combined.

We could see through the floorboards in our house. We would play underneath the house. We built playhouses and made up outdoor games from nothing because that's what we had. There were no board games or even cards. We didn't have a television or even a radio. We just had our imaginations.

I slept in one room with three of my sisters—Mina, Mary, and Cookie—in a used bed my mother had gotten from a white family whose house she cleaned. The bed was huge and it took up practically the entire room. It was a beautiful leather bed that had a bullet hole in the headboard where the lady's son had shot himself in it. But we didn't care about that. The bed was big enough for each of us to have our own space.

I always had a vision of what my perfect home, my perfect life, would be. It wasn't that this house represented our life's accomplishments. Not for me. For me, it represented home, *our* home. At last. It represented the life I had always dreamed of. It was perfection. Boy, was I wrong. Not even my dream home could save us.

In this home was where my marriage would continue to fall apart.

In addition, the move to Atlanta was undermining professionally. The church culture was different. It was a bit misogynistic. The men there believed that women needed to know their place. And I didn't fit that mold. I immediately rolled up my sleeves when we got there and started to work, building the church right alongside my husband. I took the lowly secretary's position, making $75 a week at first and eventually a whopping $250 a week. It was a huge step backward for me after leaving California, where I had been a senior engineer for the largest energy company in the state, making six figures: now, as the church secretary/administrator, I was working more hours and under more pressure.

But I was working for my family. I was working to put Dennis's career on the right path. I had negotiated Dennis's deal with the church, tying his salary to the growth of Tabernacle. By the fourth year, the church was doing so well, he was making more than $200,000 a year—which was why we could easily afford this house.

When I first got there, I worked to settle the outstanding lawsuits and tax liens the church had. I even founded a quality childcare program there.

My involvement in the church didn't sit well with some of the elders and deacons. There was a lot of talk among the deacons that I was taking over the church.

I was good at building things. I was used to organizing and running a business, and I treated the church as if it was a business . . . because it was. As the secretary/church administrator, I made a lot of changes that put the church in a position to be successful. But change is tough for people—especially when they aren't used to order. There was a lot of rebellion.

The talk was wearing on Dennis, and I know he was starting to resent me for having put him in that position. So we had a lot of things happening in our relationship at the same time. And the therapy still wasn't working.

I finally decided to tell Dr. Ashe the truth. Once that happened, she started to deal with Dennis's actions and behavior and challenge him. He didn't like that. Soon, he refused to go to therapy. I knew we were really in trouble then.

Dennis was living two lives. He lived one with me and one without me. It was a torturous kind of thing. At first he thought, the way he was, was evil. Then he transitioned into believing it was just who he was.

At first, he didn't even want to talk about it. We went to counseling, but he was never open about it. When he'd been honest in counseling in California, they told him he was sinful and evil and diseased and sick, and that he needed "curing." That judgment probably created the monster he turned out to be later. When you're trying to be something you're not, to live a life that's unnatural for you, if someone tells you enough times that you are a monster, you will soon turn into that monster.

I believe when we got married, Dennis intended to be faithful. He intended to be a good husband. Many of us believe that when we get married all and any prior unhealthy behaviors will cease—something magical will happen at the altar— because now you're with the right one. Wrong! The notion that the premarriage behavior will magically disappear is a gross misconception. The magic of the moment is just that; it's magic just for the moment—it cannot endure the test of time. Dennis just couldn't be faithful and be himself at the same time.

Eventually he chose to be himself. A painful price for both of us!

Little did I know that despite him trying to hide, all of those years, one of our sons was paying very close attention.

CHAPTER ELEVEN

The Apple and the Tree

Do not judge, or you too will be judged.
For in the same way you judge others, you will be judged.

—Matthew 7:1

When Micah was in middle school, he used to carry a notebook to school every day with a picture of his father taped to the cover. Dennis had taken some head shots and body shots early in our marriage when he was toying with the possibility of modeling. A few of the photos were of him in a tank top, showing off his bodybuilder's physique.

It was one of the muscle shots that Micah sported on the

notebook he took to middle school every day. And for three full years, he was insistent on this picture being featured on his new notebook for school.

I took it as him completely doting on his daddy. Maybe for him it was a reminder of what he'd like to become—more masculine, as his Daddy was always telling him to be, for his own protection.

Still, Micah hung out with only girls at school. He was very popular in the choral and the drama departments in middle and later in high school. Just as his brother Taylor was before him, Micah was named "Most Talented" in his high school graduating class.

He won numerous state singing competitions, and he acted and danced in many school productions.

To my surprise, Micah also went out for the track team his junior year in high school and turned out to be very athletic. He made all-state in the hurdles event, and I attended every track meet.

In his senior year, he had to choose between track and chorus. He chose chorus. I went to every one of Micah's performances. I loved seeing my children display their talents. I remember having family and friends over, and would call for Micah.

"Mickey, please come down and sing mama one of those ballads you sing, you know, from *Les Misérables*."

"No, Mom, please leave me alone," he would yell down the stairs.

I had to beg and beg until finally he would give in. And when he opened his mouth, the room stood still. The quality of his voice was better than his father's.

Micah was as smart as he was talented. He was in the Governor's Honors Program, was a Merit Scholar, and was in accelerated classes. He won a full scholarship to Shorter College—known as the Juilliard of the South—for his vocal gifts.

We were so proud of him. And he seemed to be thriving at Shorter.

It was Christmas break and Micah was in his first year of college. He had just finished his first semester. I was at the kitchen sink, cracking eggs for breakfast, and Dennis was sitting at the island reading the paper.

"I have an announcement," Micah said, still in his pajamas.

We both looked up.

"Mom and Dad, I'm gay!" he blurted out. "I know what the Bible says about it. I've been struggling with it for a while. But that's who I am."

That was his statement. It was as if he had rehearsed it for weeks and he rushed to get it out. When he was done speaking, he turned and headed to his room to get ready for breakfast. Dennis and I looked at each and didn't say a word. I finished cooking and acted as if everything was okay. I went into denial/avoid mode. And Dennis said, "Well, damn."

When Micah and his two brothers came down, we ate and

acted as if nothing had changed. The next day (giving us not a minute to digest the news), Micah brought a young man over to the house. "Mom, Dad, this is Stephen." We found out it was his boyfriend.

All I could think was, *When did this all happen?*

Quite frankly, I was stunned. Shocked. I'm rarely at a loss for words, but this whole scene sent me for a loop. The young man was white, and he looked as if he couldn't be more than fifteen. He had brown, curly hair and these big, light-brown eyes. We were all very uncomfortable. But we were hospitable and friendly—Southern hospitality at its best.

He and Micah went out and sat by the pool. Dennis and I just watched them from the gathering room.

"Well, he didn't give us much time to get ready for this," Dennis said.

After Micah came home from hanging out with Stephen, I took him out for lunch. I wanted to talk with him one-on-one. We went to our local Chick-fil-A, of all places. Micah had worked there when he was in high school. I told him he needed to be careful, and I talked to him about the risks of HIV and other STDs. He was only eighteen, and I knew that young people seem to think they are invincible. I wanted him to be armed with all the information he needed. That was my response to most problems—research and study. I always believed that knowledge was power.

"Mom, don't worry about me. I got this," he said.

I knew that, as a gay man, he was struggling with the tension between his faith and his acceptance of his sexuality, and this bothered me perhaps more than him being gay. I set up an appointment to speak with my therapist, Dr. Ashe. She had already helped me get through so much with Dennis. At this point, Dr. Ashe was my personal therapist and was on speed dial. I was talking with her more than with my family or friends. And I needed every minute of our time together. It seemed that as soon as I came to grips with one bit of drama—Dennis being arrested, admitting he was bisexual, or giving me a venereal disease—I was hit with another. Like my son now declaring that he was also gay.

To be honest, I was struggling mentally and emotionally. Had I done something wrong? How could I protect my son? And what did his being gay mean for his future? I didn't care about what preachers said the Bible predicted would be his eternal future—that never touched my consciousness. I was concerned about my son's survival in a world that hated gay folk and believed they were insane.

In my heart, in my spirit, I didn't believe my son was insane or doomed to eternal damnation. But I needed to talk it out, think it out—I needed to talk to Dr. Ashe.

What I knew for a fact was that Micah was different from the day he was born. I remembered the day he was born. He was the prettiest baby. Not just handsome; Micah was pretty and gentle in his demeanor. Taylor, our firstborn, was rugged and low maintenance. Micah wanted to be held, carried, and cuddled all the time.

I noticed that he was effeminate before his first birthday. We took a family portrait. The two boys were sitting side by side with Dennis and me posing behind them. The photographer positioned the boys' hands folded in their laps. Micah's hands drooped at the wrists. Both of his wrists were bent naturally. He wasn't even a year old.

When I looked at the photo, all I could say in my spirit— not out loud—was *Oh my God, what could this mean?* It just looked weird. Little things like that were there all along, if I reflected back. Even his touch was different than Taylor's touch. It was so gentle and soft. As Micah got older, it became more apparent that he was probably gay. But it wasn't something I ever wanted to confront him about or discuss.

When we were in California, Dennis would scold Micah about his effeminate mannerisms. "Do you want people to think you are gay?" he would say. I didn't stop Dennis from scolding him, because I think I was afraid for him and wanted it to stop. The kids at school were already constantly teasing him, calling him *faggot* and things like that. I wanted him to be accepted and have a normal childhood.

I later found out that in addition to the teasing, he had been molested when he was ten at church by one of the teen boys. All of this came out when he came out. He didn't feel that he could tell us that then. While we were spending so much time being the perfect family to the world, there was really a lot going on that I quite simply wasn't paying attention to. I felt like a complete failure. My child had been suffering through something, and I hadn't seen it and I didn't know it. I hadn't been there to protect him. He'd suffered in silence, and that completely broke my heart.

Micah was sitting in the basement, one of his favorite places to be, and I came down to sit right next to him.

"How's mama's baby?" I asked.

He just smiled that sweet, gentle, warm smile and gave me a hug.

"Whatcha thinking about?"

"Nothing really, Mom."

"Mickey, when did it start? How did you know you were gay?" I wanted to know.

He avoided that question and hit me with this:

"Mom, no one ever messed with Taylor. They just messed with me. That's why I would always tell on him when he got into trouble at school. I was kind of mad that no one ever messed with him. Why did they leave him alone? Why did they only mess with me?"

Mess with him? I had no idea what he was talking about.

"What do you mean?"

"Mom, do you remember Joe Davis from MBC?"

"Yes . . ."

"He would take me to an isolated place and mess with me." He wouldn't look at me. He kept his head down as he was telling me.

I had an OMG look on my face.

"He touched my private area, Mom, and I liked it."

The "liked it" part escaped me. All I could think about at that moment was that a grown man (he was eighteen at the time) had been touching my baby.

Because I am so transparent, Micah saw I was pissed to high heaven.

"Mom, I liked it," he said again, nearly on the verge of tears.

"Mickey, you were just a *kid*."

"But Mom, I *liked* it."

Micah had been carrying around so many emotional burdens for so long. So when he finally did talk to us, I guess he just wanted to get it all out and move on. My first instinct was to get him help. I wanted him to speak to someone. But he kept insisting that he was fine.

We had to deal with it. I didn't understand what kind of life Micah would have as a gay man. As far as his spiritual life, I didn't consider whether being gay was a sin, and I didn't care.

In California, when Dennis was going through his "sex addiction," with men, I learned that there were many teachings on homosexuality. That was the first time I heard that it was a sin. Growing up in Macon, sex in general was taboo. So "homo sex" was not mentioned either. My childhood pastor never preached on the subject. Dealing with folks from Focus on the Family, I learned that homosexuality was not just a sin, but that it was an abomination. I personally never believed that. It was what Focus on the Family preached on their radio show in California, where Dennis and I learned of the gay detox camp.

With Dennis, I believed it was a sickness, like alcoholism, or a condition, like being born blind. I believed it was something that could be controlled with counseling and/or something that couldn't be helped, especially as it related to my husband, who I later discovered had been struggling with his own sexuality even before he met me.

Dennis's infidelities with men and the counseling we received in California caused me to believe that this condition of "being gay/bisexual" could be fixed. I believed that God had ordained my marriage. And that anything that threatened my marriage was wrong. In this context, I judged my husband. I judged Dennis's condition on this basis, rather than believe the truth, because I couldn't bear the pain of what this truth would mean for our marriage. Because if my husband was gay, then there would be no hope for our marriage, and I wasn't ready to deal with that. I had suffered so much pain already.

But now my son was saying that he was gay. This was my child. My baby.

I now needed to know the truth, no matter how much it hurt. I needed answers. When I spoke to Dr. Ashe about it, she talked to me about the science behind homosexuality. She talked about the research on homosexuality, and the findings of the American Psychological Association and the American Psychiatric Association, whose scientific research explained that it was neither a choice nor a sickness nor insanity that needed to be treated. It wasn't something that could be "prayed away" or reversed. She said that, in fact, homosexuality was quite normal.

Normal?

How could that be? Tension hit me from all directions— tension from the biblical text and tension from my gut. The biblical text did not completely inform my faith tradition, but my experience with God ultimately shaped my views. I believed somebody somewhere was screwing everybody else around with these notions of condemnation. However, acquitting my son or my husband of a so-called sin was not my agenda. My agenda was saving my son and my marriage. I found out that I couldn't do both. When I set Micah free and accepted the truth about his homosexuality, my marriage was over.

I started my journey to discover the truth with a deep-seated conviction that I could save my family and keep it intact. I never for one moment thought that this road would actually lead to the demise of my marriage.

My only thought was Micah. I would love him through

this. Make him feel safe. Make him feel accepted. A mother's instinct is to protect. That is what love does, if it's pure. It protects.

I told myself that I would not oppress or ostracize my child. I would get educated and understand him. I was going to love him, no matter what. But loving him was not enough. I needed to understand him, and I needed him to know that I supported him, no matter what.

I went to a gay bookstore in Midtown Atlanta and inquired about books on this subject. The store owner suggested I start with Mel White's *Stranger at the Gate*. This book really opened my eyes. I saw my son and my husband on every page.

Mel White declared that you *can* love the Lord; you can serve the Lord *and* also be gay. It wasn't a spiritual death sentence. Mel White initially believed that it was, so he tried everything to "un-gay" himself. He had been through electric shock therapy. He had gone through the Exodus program, and when he was done with all of that, he was still gay. Mel White finally came to a place of acceptance. He knew two things: God made him, and God loved him. And that was affirmation for me!

Despite bigoted biblical "interpretations" that condemn same-gender loving people, the truth is, God is love, God is forgiveness, and God is acceptance. I knew in my gut that love trumps negative rhetoric, faith hate, and bigotry.

My son would take a long journey before he believed this

truth. It's always harder for the victim of hate to accept that they are loved and accepted. Micah had lived the scorn, he'd lived the teasing and ridicule, he'd lived with the pronouncements of doom. I was his mother, telling him that he was okay and why. But he had to know this for himself.

Then I started to think of how harshly I'd treated Dennis—not caring what he had suffered during childhood and throughout adulthood. I had only cared about myself and how his sexuality had affected our marriage and my life. I thought about all of the mothers and fathers who tossed their children (some fifteen years old and younger) out on the streets, disowning them, because they found out they were gay. I thought about Dennis's fear of his father and how he had to hide because if he gave an inkling of his true self it would have been a death sentence, in the context of his family. I thought about the choices he'd made and the internal conflict he endured daily as a preacher, socially and emotionally railroaded into heterosexual relationships and ultimately marriage when he was a bisexual man. I thought of all of the so-called Christians who played judge and jury, sentencing thousands and thousands of people to a living hell here on earth. And they did that while wearing their WWJD (what would Jesus do) bracelets.

The hypocrites: I was one of them.

So, I made a decision. I was going to love and accept not just my son but anyone I came in contact with. I was not just going to spread love, I was going to preach about it and teach it.

I know that there are so many mothers and fathers, sisters and brothers, so many children themselves who are suffering, thinking that God said that homosexuality is a sin and that everyone who is a homosexual is going to hell.

Every Mother's Day, Dennis would ask me to preach. The Mother's Day after Micah came out, I preached about parenting (edifying and encouraging) children who are different—even children who are gay. I know it made Dennis uncomfortable, because he had yet to publicly address his own homosexuality and was still big on image. But I preached the sermon boldly, and it got a standing ovation. The tide began to turn with Dennis.

We started talking more, and I saw that some of our discussions would end up being sermon content. I taught a Bible study series at the church from Daniel Helminiak's book *What the Bible Really Says About Homosexuality*. The congregation's gay members began to grow, and the church had a new tagline and mission—love and acceptance. Tabernacle Baptist Church: A Place of Love and Acceptance.

I was doing all of this to pave the way for Micah to accept himself. He would be there in the Bible studies and for the sermons, but he still wasn't ready to let go of his self-loathing. No matter how much I tried to reach him with positive reflections about his sexuality, he continued to deflect.

"I love you," he would say. "Thanks, Mom!"

But they were just words. I knew he was still hurting. Micah had to live in the greater society that held beliefs much different from those held by his parents. And his father was still a closeted man. The family hypocrisy blocked the reckoning of his truth. Dennis was hiding his true identity, teaching a doctrine of love and acceptance but did not love and accept himself. He needed his father's affirmation to walk proudly in his truth, an affirmation that came too late and at a great price.

CHAPTER TWELVE

The Diagnosis I

I was sitting in the living room of my sister Faye's house in Florida. I would go hang out with my baby sister frequently, especially during this period when Dennis and I were going through so many ups and downs. This was one of those periods when I was really feeling down.

Faye was the maid of honor in my wedding. I would come down to work on her computers for her hair salons—All Dolled Up—and share the drama in my life. She would share her drama, and we would pray together and cry together. Cry and pray. Pray and cry. And I'd go to the beach to see God's face.

Whenever I'd return home from Florida, I would have the emotional and spiritual strength to face my next challenge. Faye was my favorite sister (of course, I say this to all my sisters).

The phone rang while I was lounging on her couch in the living room. It was Dennis. I was surprised because he didn't normally contact me when I was at Faye's house. He knew that was my time to be away from him. Besides, we weren't on good terms at this point. He was back to hanging out late, giving me lame excuses and outright lies and refusing to go back to therapy. I wasn't really speaking to him. So for him to call, I knew something was wrong.

"Mickey is positive," was all Dennis said.

He just blurted it out with no setup.

It took me a minute to register that he wasn't talking about my son's sunny personality. Positive? I can't tell you what else he said, if anything, because I went completely numb. While I wanted it to be a lie, I knew that my son was indeed *HIV*-positive. It was what I feared would happen, when Micah first came out to me as gay, just a few years before. It was why I sat him down and talked to him about safe sex, got him pamphlets, talked to him about the importance of condoms. I knew the possibilities. Now the possibility was a reality.

I hung up the phone and caught the first flight back to Georgia.

When I got home, Micah was in his room. He looked like he had been crying for days. And when he saw me, he just cried harder. I just held him. I held my baby.

In my spirit, I said, *My baby is not going to die.*

Between the 1980s and 1990s, people who had AIDS were dying the most horrific deaths. They were dying quickly and they were dying with lesions and extreme weight loss, and often alone. What made having the disease even more challenging was not just battling the symptoms, the complications, and the actual deterioration of your health; it was also the stigma that came with HIV. It was called the gay disease. And people felt that whoever had it deserved to have it, and deserved to die. This meant that they were saying my baby deserved to die!

There were those like Ryan White and Elizabeth Glaser who had contracted it through a blood transfusion. And of course, there was Magic Johnson, a married, heterosexual basketball superstar who contracted the virus through extra-marital heterosexual sex. But those cases were not the norm, and they weren't what people saw when they thought about HIV and AIDS. What they saw was the gay guy played by Tom Hanks in *Philadelphia*.

AIDS was a vicious disease and had a lot of hate associated with it—even in the faith community. There were those who believed it was a curse, a plague from God against homosexuals, and that those who had it deserved what they got.

I told my baby, "You're not going to die like that. You're not going out like that!" And I meant it.

The whole family was in the room, embracing him, all of us crying with him. At that point, none of us had any words. We were just there for him—just present.

When Dennis and his brothers left, I stayed. All I could do was lie there in the bed with Micah and hold him as he cried like a baby—nonstop tears.

When Micah finally spoke, he said, "Mom, you know how they die? You know how they look when they die?"

"You're not going to look like that, Mickey," I said with every fiber of my body. "You're not going to die. You're not going to die like that. You're going to live. You're going to be fine. Now, you believe that. You're my son!

"I prayed for you since you were in my womb and that is *not* going to happen to you."

Micah was inconsolable. He turned to drugs. He began to stay out later and later. He kept up his schoolwork, but his nightlife escalated. He went from hanging out on the weekends to hanging out every night of the week.

Dennis had bought the boys their own cars while they were in college. So Micah had transportation to go anywhere he wanted to go without any policing from his parents. I felt so helpless and stressed.

I did what I always did to cope with stress—work more and sleep more. So I wasn't aware to what extent Micah was staying out, and I didn't notice the drug use at all. But Dennis did. Dennis was a night owl. He was either out or up!

And Dennis being the dad he has always been—attentive and concerned—was the one to intervene.

One night Micah came home, and his father met him at the door.

"If you don't stop using drugs, you're getting out of this house and I'm taking my hands off of you," he warned Micah.

I later found out that Micah was smoking cigarettes and weed and doing Ecstasy. Micah idolized his daddy, so Dennis's words cut him. And Micah listened.

He stopped using drugs immediately, cold turkey, and started to put his life back together. Dennis made him assistant director of the choir. This helped to change Micah's mind-set. He started to talk to us and share what he was going through.

In one of these moments, he told me who had infected him. It was an older white man.

"Mommy, I know exactly who it was and when it happened," he said.

"Well, you can't undo it," I told him. "Stop thinking about the past, son."

But in my heart, I wished I could get my hands on that joker!

We had a ministry for HIV and AIDS victims at the church. So Micah saw firsthand how people with the disease were treated. People with AIDS were ostracized. When people found out someone had the disease, they didn't want to be around that person. They didn't want to touch you or treat you. It was played out in the movie *Philadelphia*, but Micah was seeing it in real life, in church, in members who were living with the disease.

Back then, there were so many misconceptions and lies about how the disease could be contracted. People were so ignorant, and some would treat victims as if they were lepers.

Micah kept his status a secret, so he would not "directly" experience the shame. I tried to soothe him. I would hug and kiss him as much as I could. I would eat off his plate to show him I wasn't afraid of his disease. I wore him out with attention. But it wasn't enough.

Micah was suffering from more than HIV. It was guilt. It was hiding. It was shame. Micah wanted to keep this secret. He didn't want us to tell a soul—not even our extended family. Micah, like millions of gay men around the world, was feeling as if he wasn't accepted—he felt hopeless.

He made us promise not to tell anyone—not even our families. I don't know what kind of conversations he was having with his father. I think Dennis was starting to have conversations with Micah about how he was living, about his sexuality. I think Micah's HIV diagnosis changed Dennis. While Micah refused to tell the truth about what he was enduring—for years—it seemed to free Dennis. It may have given him the courage to really live his truth.

Dennis was still in the closet at this point. He was telling people that the only reason he was preaching about homosexuality and acceptance was because his son was gay.

CHAPTER THIRTEEN

The Diagnosis II

Dennis had been suffering from a terrible case of psoriasis, which started at the top of 2005, while we were traveling promoting a CD—*Live on Sunday at Tabernacle*—that had been produced by our son Taylor. It was the church's first recording, and Dennis's first solo album. While on the road, we had gotten word that Dennis's father had taken a turn for the worse.

Big June had become ill in October of 2004. He drove himself to the emergency room because he did not feel well.

After being examined, he was admitted into the hospital. They discovered he had cancer in his lungs and in his abdomen. Big June remained hospitalized for two months. In January of 2005, he was moved to hospice. The doctors had done all they could do; the cancer had spread and surgery would not improve his condition. On March 1, 2005, Big June passed away. Mom (Dennis's mother) recounted that in the four months of Big June's illness, Dennis traveled home to Toledo at least fifteen times. It was clear that Dennis had a great bond with his father, and his father's transition was a tremendous and painful loss.

Dennis's family was emotionally crippled. They left everything for Dennis to take care of—everything. His father must have known that Dennis would be the only one to come through, because he left him with that responsibility in his will. Big June was proud of Dennis because Dennis had finished college and stayed married and raised his sons under the same roof. His other sons had multiple women, multiple children with different women, and none were married. A couple of his brothers even battled substance abuse. Dennis was the one Big June trusted. Dennis was the executor of his estate. He was in charge, but I supported and helped him with every detail, including the funeral arrangements.

The funeral home did a great job with the body. The church where Big June's funeral service was held was one of those old Baptist church buildings, like the one where Whitney

Houston's service was held, with high, cathedral ceilings, antique architecture, and great acoustics. It was huge, and the church was packed with all of June's family and friends—the Harley biker friends, the "other" women, and his old hangout buddies. June didn't go to church, but he sure filled one at his home-going service. And the Meredith clan was huge.

Dennis preached his father's eulogy. The title of the sermon was "The Power of a Good Name." He preached about the virtue of having a good name and took his text from Proverbs 3:3–4. But what stood out for me was the emotion evoked by the service and Dennis's powerful sermon.

Dennis is like a soldier on the battlefield when he hits the pulpit in terms of courage and stamina. All of his life events and emotions are poured out from the pulpit. There is no fear and no filter. When Dennis preaches, he is phenomenal. That's one of the things I absolutely love about him. In that pulpit, Dennis is pure power and strength.

He grieved for his father in private. Dennis was not only suffering emotionally, he was also a complete mess, with his hands afflicted with psoriasis. He was restless and distant during this entire time. But when he said good-bye officially to his dad, he was the picture of strength.

After we got back home, Dennis was a different man.

He complained that he couldn't get enough rest sleeping with me, so he moved to the other upstairs bedroom. We would sleep together after date night on Fridays.

Dennis was no longer present. He wasn't present as a husband, and during this period, he wasn't even present as a father. The older boys had both graduated from college and were living in our condo, and both were still working at Tabernacle. Eddie, who had finished high school in 2003, was still in college, doing well, and still at home.

In January 2006, Dennis was downstairs working on his Sunday sermon and discovered a lump under his arm. He came upstairs to show me.

"Lydia, look at this."

"Wow," I said, because it looked pretty significant.

"When did you notice this?"

Dennis responded, "Just now."

"It's probably nothing," I said, not wanting him to worry.

"But I'll call Dr. Mack to make an appointment for you early next week."

We went to the doctor and they suggested a biopsy. The biopsy results came back and Dennis was diagnosed with Hodgkin's lymphoma. It was a rare form of cancer, and it had already spread. However, the doctor said it would be easy to treat.

Dennis was devastated. This is where my ability to deny and suppress emotion came in handy. I jumped into fix-it mode. I was there for him the entire way, researching the disease and looking for other treatment options. We entertained the thought of holistic medical treatments, but the doctors laughed at us about even the thought of this notion. Dennis ended up having rounds and rounds of chemotherapy. It was awful.

While I was there to support him, he seemed to not want me there. Dennis purchased another condo in May of 2006, which was within walking distance of my school. He announced that with all he was going through, he thought it would be best for him to move into the condo for a while. He explained, "I think this will help us with our marriage, and give me a chance to rediscover what we lost." He never invited me to the condo during his cancer treatments.

He seemed to be fishing for excuses. He also said that the smells in the house—cleaning products and potpourri—were making him even more nauseous. He also said he didn't want me seeing him so sick.

Dennis was telling me everything . . . but the truth.

After Dennis's first cancer treatment, we promised to pick Micah up and take him house hunting. On our way, Dennis and I got into a heated argument outside of the condo complex where Micah and Taylor lived, over him telling a church member we were separated, which was news to me.

"Dennis, why in the world would you tell Eric we are living in separate homes?!"

Eric was a member of the church who had come to see him during his chemo treatment.

"You always try to make me feel like I can't lead my

church," he said, which wasn't even the issue. I was fighting mad. It wasn't just about me saving face. A leak about a separation between the pastor and his wife would start an uproar in the church, especially among his enemies. Tabernacle was becoming known as a church that welcomed people from the lesbian, gay, bisexual, and transgender communities, since Micah came out and the ministry of Love and Acceptance was fully launched.

But many of the older members were not pleased. Not at all. Dennis was holding on to the heterosexual membership by a thin thread. Our marriage was holding on by an even thinner thread.

Dennis's treatments were difficult. He was very emotional and sometimes even tearful. He had lost a lot of weight and was really struggling through it. I was determined to be there with him despite him pushing me away every chance he got.

Although it was making him very sick, Dennis responded well to the chemo. It seemed to be working. He was scheduled to have his last treatment in June. His mother wanted to come and be with him through it all, but he didn't want her there. He didn't want her seeing him in such a weakened state, he said. After all she had been through with his dad, whom she had finally left and divorced, after years of abuse, before he got sick. But Dennis couldn't stop Mom. She was determined to be there for his last treatment. But, in my heart, I knew Dennis did not want to tell his mother that we were separated.

I absolutely love Dennis's mother. She was the best mother-in-law any woman could imagine. She was there for the birth of each of our children. She even kept them in the summers. She was a shoulder to cry on. And while I never told her the truth about our marriage while I was going through it, she was more supportive than she ever knew.

When Mom arrived, she immediately knew something was wrong beyond his health. He finally had to tell his mother that we were separated. I told him I wasn't telling her, that it had been his decision to live apart from me, and therefore his responsibility to tell his mother. I wasn't there for the conversation, but I know from her that he told her that the decision to separate was mutual. A lie. He also told her he was tired of the constant arguing. Another lie.

She was always very loving toward me, and she didn't care if Dennis and I were together or not. I was still her only daughter.

Every day Dennis, who refused to invite his mother to his condo, would come back to the house, where she was staying with me, to spend time with her. When Dennis left, we sat around and talked for hours. I cleared up all of the lies Dennis had told her. Then I told her the truth: that her son was bisexual/gay.

She shared with me that she had suspected that Dennis was gay for a long time, since he was a teenager. She cried a lot that weekend. We both did. We talked the way I wished we had talked all along. We were raw and honest.

"When you came into his life, you were the answer to my prayers," she told me as we sat on the couch together in the family room. We were on that couch for hours.

She thought Dennis had found the one who could change him. She had hoped that, being with me—and he seemed so happy with me—he would walk away from that homosexual lifestyle. She had hoped that I would be the answer, the cure.

Dennis's mom was so hurt for me and for the family. She didn't want me to be a "wife reject." Mom said that after her divorce from Big June, she'd felt like a wife reject. She asked me if I thought that Dennis was really called by God to preach. I thought about it.

"Yes, he is," I said. "And he's also gay."

"Dennis being gay does not mean that he cannot be used or called by God."

That Sunday when we went to church, Mom told me she scoped out the situation and had a revelation.

"Sweets [her nickname for me], the man Dennis is sleeping with is close," she said. "He is in the church. You've probably seen him. You probably know him."

One minute later, Dennis called for children's church to exit. And Lamont Golden was the next face I saw. I gazed at him and then looked away.

After Mom left for home, I left too. I went to Florida to stay with my sister. I needed the mental rest. When I came back, Dennis picked me up from the airport. I could tell while

I was in Florida he was feeling better. He seemed to be having a great time in my absence. I knew something was up, because he was being too nice.

I had been begging him to let the school use the church van to pick up children who needed transportation. On the drive home, he told me that he would allow it. I just looked at him with deep suspicion, thinking, *What is going to happen next?*

We would often counsel members in our church about their relationships, which increasingly became ridiculous for me to do, as we were clearly not role models. That Sunday, we had an appointment with a couple after church. Two gay women requested us to come to their home for the session.

While I was driving us to their home, Dennis said to me, "I think I want to live the rest of my life as a gay man."

Now, I was driving, and this man was telling me our marriage was over. I almost ran off the road. I guess I should have seen it coming, but I couldn't see straight. I arrived at the counseling session and went through it on autopilot. We counseled the couple and drove home in silence.

The whole time Dennis was being treated for cancer with chemotherapy, he treated me like a stranger, and he was very mean. But still I never left his side. *Through sickness and in health* was what I was thinking.

Then I took a three-day break in Florida and he arrived at a decision to officially end our marriage? I returned to the house that Sunday to find Taylor moving the rest of Dennis's things. When he'd decided we needed a little break he'd only taken a few things, giving me hope that he would be returning. Now he was clearing out everything that was his.

He'd had affairs all throughout our marriage. But none of them had resulted in him being mean to me or distant. We were still able to connect, laugh, and be a family. In fact, as I reflected on our marriage, during some of his most philandering years, he was most attentive to me—especially in the bedroom.

His cheating never meant distancing himself from me, which was why I never suspected. He never missed a beat in our home—not with our children and not with me.

Now he was a different man. I didn't recognize him. At first, I chalked it up to the cancer. But if I thought about it, he'd really been distant before the diagnosis. It had to be another person. I asked him if that was it.

"No," he said emphatically. "I just want to live my life the way I am—as a gay man."

"But if there is no one else, why does it matter?" I asked.

"I just want to be true to myself," he said.

"There is someone else," I told him. "I feel it."

"No, there is no one else." He kept denying it.

I knew he was lying.

CHAPTER FOURTEEN

The End

In July, rumors were flying around my childcare center that one of my teachers was sleeping with my husband. I told Dennis about it and he laughed it off. He denied the rumors profusely.

This preschool teacher he was supposedly sleeping with was someone Dennis had asked me to hire. He had brought this person into my home for dinner. He had invited this person to lead the children's ministry at the church. There was some connection between Dennis and this person. And this person had been seen around town in Dennis's car with him. So I figured there must be something to these rumors.

But Dennis still emphatically denied he was dating anyone—and definitely not Lamont.

I still had my suspicions. In the past, Dennis had a habit of bringing home lovers of his (unbeknownst to me, of course). There was one guy who was there so much that I came home from work one evening and he was there in my kitchen with my apron on, cooking spaghetti for my family. Dennis tried to make sure I was friendly with his boyfriends so that I wouldn't be suspicious.

But since he had confessed he had done this in the past, I was now even more suspicious when rumors began swirling about Lamont.

The whole thing came to a head when Lamont was given a disciplinary action from the senior director of my childcare for poor job performance. Dennis had begged me to hire him. But Lamont wasn't fulfilling the responsibility of his job, nor did he seem to have the knowledge or background to run a classroom. Then I found out that he'd asked one of my clients to defend him in a case. He was being sued by his previous employer for falsifying his credentials as a lead Georgia pre-K teacher. Livid, the client reported the incident to my senior director. My senior director suspended him for inappropriate conduct and for poor job performance. Lamont then turned in his resignation.

Things just weren't lining up. Why would Dennis want an inexperienced, incompetent, unethical person working with our kids at my school and at the church? Why? Unless there was something more to their relationship? After I found out that Lamont had been fired from his previous job, I confronted Dennis again. And again he denied any personal involvement with this man—this *young* man. He was in his twenties.

The same week, I had an issue with Lamont's assistant teacher. I reprimanded her, and she didn't like it and blamed Lamont. She then proceeded to tell me how Lamont had bragged about sleeping with my husband and that Dennis had frequently invited her and Lamont to lunch at his condo, which was within walking distance of my school. This rang true to me, because Dennis never invited me to his condo.

I called Dennis immediately, blowing up his phone until he finally picked up. I was very upset.

"Tell me the truth!" I said.

He finally did. He told me that he was having an affair with Lamont. He told me that he'd met him at a jack-off club around Thanksgiving the year before. *Thanksgiving?* It had been going on that long? I felt dead. Mom was right: Dennis's lover had been staring me in the face the whole time.

"How could you do this to me?!" I was hysterical at this point.

How could he bring this person into my home, into my

workplace, into the lives of my family, into the church, into my personal space? How could he disrespect me like this?

I hung up the phone.

Dennis kept texting me apologizing and asking me to let him explain. I had no words for Dennis. I couldn't even stand the sight or thought of him. His voice, even his face disgusted me. I felt as if he was driving a car and "aiming" to run me over. And that he kept running me over, again and again, even though I was already down. Everything in me died. It was the worst pain in my whole life. My heart was completely broken.

And so was my family.

I drove straight to my sister Tricia's house. I started crying as soon as she opened the door. She let me cry for a minute and then she said, "This is about Dennis being gay, isn't it?"

What?

I had never discussed his sexuality with anyone in my family. I was too embarrassed. Everyone thought he might have been cheating on me with women. But I'd never brought up the bisexuality or the homosexuality.

"How did you know?" I asked her.

"I heard some men talking in the corridor at your wedding," she said. "They were wondering why Dennis was marrying a woman."

"Tricia," I said, "why didn't you tell me?"

"I knew you wouldn't have listened. You needed to find out

for yourself. I just didn't think it would take this long," she said.

I spent the night with Tricia that night, telling her that I'd known for a while. And, like she always did, she licked my wounds. Then she told me flatly and boldly: "Get over it!"

She wasn't going to let me have that pity party of mine for very long. I needed to get it together and put back the pieces of my broken life.

When Dennis left in 2005, my baby Eddie was nineteen years old. He had failed out of two colleges and entered the navy, where he was honorably discharged after just a year. Eddie took our split the hardest. He was there to see it all unravel.

He began to really act out and was very disrespectful to his father.

"You ain't shit," he told him one evening. "Why would you do this to my mother?!"

Eddie doted on me and constantly asked if I was all right. But he wasn't all right. He was emotionally a wreck.

Micah was pissed and wanted to beat up Lamont. Taylor covered up for his dad—as I discovered he had been doing the whole time. Taylor and Micah were already grown and living their lives, but the separation affected us all. Taylor had finished college with a degree in music engineering at Georgia State University. Micah, who was doing well on his meds and living a full life with HIV, had also graduated from Georgia State University, with a degree in religion. They were both working in the church.

Micah still kept his status a secret, even though I encouraged him to tell, because every time he and his boyfriend had a fight, the boyfriend would threaten to tell.

"You don't want anyone to have that kind of power over you," I told him.

But he wasn't ready to share what he felt was the worst thing that could happen to anyone, with his choir or anyone else. He would take his chances that his boyfriend was bluffing.

I felt in my heart, however, that his boyfriend had already told people and that everyone already knew. But Micah, like his dad, was in denial.

What we missed most as a family through this drama was our traditions of mealtime, always eating together every evening. Vacations! And especially holiday celebrations. It was all upended.

All three of the boys were concerned about me. They knew how devoted I was to our family and their father. And I couldn't hide my devastation.

Dr. Ashe insisted that the boys should know the source of the marital tension, and if Dennis refused to tell them, then I had to. Dennis refused. So I sat my boys down individually and told them that their father was gay. Taylor and Micah already knew.

When I told Eddie, his response was, "Dad is a freak! But he has always been a loving father, and I still love him."

Knowing that their dad was gay did not hurt my children. It was the leaving that hurt.

While this wasn't the first or second or even third time I had been betrayed by Dennis, all the other times had felt like just sex. Part of his addiction. Something I could deal with because he was committed to the marriage. At least, he'd said all he wanted was our marriage and his family. He certainly never moved away from us.

But with our boys grown, and him having this condo and new freedom, I guess Dennis felt like he could really do what he wanted.

I think another thing that sealed the deal was the death of Dennis's dad. Big June was a man who instilled fear in all his sons, in everyone around him. He was a man's man, and a womanizer who was unapologetic. He expected a lot from his boys, and none of them had amounted to much of anything in June's view, except for Dennis. Dennis lived to please his daddy and make him proud.

Living a gay lifestyle wasn't an option as long as Big June was alive.

I knew the marriage was in deep trouble when Big June got really sick. Things started to change. Even when Dennis was at the height of prowling for sex in those jack-off clubs in California, he never missed a beat at home. He never missed an opportunity to make love to me and make me feel like the center of his universe, which is why it was so hard for me to accept that he was gay. How could he make love to me the way he did and be gay?

But leading up to the death of his dad, Dennis became distant in every way. We hadn't had sex in so long, I'm too embarrassed to say. He said I had humiliated him during intercourse when he couldn't get an erection one time. I figured it was midlife, and Dennis had led a promiscuous life. The erectile dysfunction was the outcome. I bought books. I offered to go to counseling. He resisted any form of outside help. Instead, he just avoided it altogether.

It seemed that my loyalty to him, commitment to him, and persistence to work things out only annoyed him.

I asked Dr. Ashe to host a family meeting. We were all there, and everyone got a chance to speak. After all the drama we had been through as a family, the boys still wanted reconciliation for their parents. They all voiced their disapproval of Dennis's boyfriend. Dennis shared his commitment to Lamont, saying he was finally in a healthy, committed, monogamous relationship—living his truth and practicing safe sex.

These words were chilling and final to me. It felt as if I had permanently lost my family by the end of the session. All Dennis could focus on was his new life and his freedom, not how he was destroying our family. In the end, despite everyone's outrage over what he was doing, there was no turning back. Dennis was moving on to this new life.

I was most concerned about Micah. He was the most involved in the church as one of the choir directors and had idolized his father. I sat there wondering what was worse for him—being HIV positive, seeing his father in a committed relationship with a man, or losing his family?

I felt powerless to help him or his brothers feel better. All I could do for my sons, and the hundreds of other church congregants who saw me as a mother, was be a positive support, an encourager, be strong in the Lord and not flounder.

Dennis often called me Mother Teresa (scornfully) because I would always try to help anybody who hurt in any way. I would spend my whole paycheck helping someone if I could. And I would freely be there with big hugs and lots of love.

I'd always been there for everyone. Now I felt completely alone. And this was not where I wanted to be. I was ashamed. And I was a wife reject!

CHAPTER FIFTEEN

Schooling

Dennis had insisted on selling the house in Fayetteville while the boys were in college. We bought a condo because of the commute. But I was fine with the commute. But he insisted we sell the house, saying that the boys—the older two of whom were still in college at the time—shouldn't have to drive so far to come home anytime they wanted.

"We need a place closer to the city," he said.

As always, I went along with the program.

The boys hated the move. I hated to leave my dream house. But Dennis bought a house in the city on Somerset Terrace. We (Eddie, Dennis, and I) moved into the house in 2004, and Dennis moved out of the house in 2005 into a new condo he bought for himself.

After Dennis left for good, I moved out of our master suite. It was very spacious, with a walk-in closet, a beautiful king-size bed. There was a sunken garden tub, a shower with a bench, and a double sink. There was a sitting area with a view of the city and hardwood floors. This was my sanctuary. But Dr. Ashe recommended that I move out of that room. I didn't understand the logic of it, but I followed her instructions. I guess she wanted me to release the last bit of my previous life with Dennis as a way of starting fresh.

She told me to change beds. In changing beds, I would change my perspective. I moved out of the room and made that my office and moved into one of the spare bedrooms—a small room across the hall from Eddie's room.

I was having trouble sleeping in the new room—my mind kept racing; it just wouldn't shut down. Dr. Ashe wanted to put me on sleep medication. But I refused and started exercising more rigorously and took long warm baths before bed. That seemed to help a little. I had so much shame around our split that I just couldn't shut off my brain to rest.

I did do one empowering thing. I filed for divorce in 2007. When I had Dennis served with divorce papers, he had the nerve to tell me that God told him it wasn't time to divorce. I don't know what God he was speaking to, but I knew in my spirit it was past time. I believe Dennis would have been content for us to stay married on paper until the day he died. As long as he could do whatever he wanted and live however he wanted, he was fine.

But I was far from fine.

Like most divorces, ours was awful. Dennis also had the nerve to refuse spousal support. I hadn't been making money for years; I had basically been volunteering my services to help Dennis build Tabernacle. I'd put off my career and my dreams for his. And he wanted to deny me support?

Dennis tried to get a member of the church who was a lawyer to represent him, but she refused. He ended up getting a high-powered attorney who never lost a case. My lawyer worked for what I could afford—pro bono. I couldn't believe Dennis was actually fighting me on this after such outright infidelity.

After spending more than $20,000, he lost his case. And he was even more combative.

The divorce was finalized in 2008, but I was still carrying around this feeling of shame. Wife reject. As if somehow something was wrong with me. Perhaps that was why I stayed so long. It wasn't that I was so forgiving—I just didn't want to be a failure.

It really makes you feel bad about who you are when you

have to admit that you can't fix everything, or when you come to the realization that your husband has moved on.

The rejection itself makes you feel worthless.

I was thinking about how embarrassed I was. My marriage had failed. And everybody knew what he'd done. How stupid I'd been. It was a strange set of emotions. But I knew that shame was one of them. I really was embarrassed about how I had let myself be treated as less than a human being. But Dennis was able to walk about as if nothing had happened.

After work, the hardest thing in the world was to come home to an empty house. I would come upstairs and take a bath. I would sit in that tub and pray that the pain and hurt would just wash away. I was seeking some kind of rest in my spirit and to free my mind. I felt as if I was having a nervous breakdown.

I felt alone in my room in my twin bed. I'd lie there and do the only thing I knew I could. Pray.

My mother taught us how to pray when we were very young. And I never forgot it. No matter what it was, no matter how small the matter, Mother told us that prayer was the answer.

"Prayer is just like you're talking to me," she would say. "But you're talking to God and telling God what's wrong. And you trust that it will be all right. You just trust in God, and God will make it all right."

I learned that at six years old and have carried it with me through my whole life. I knew prayer would carry me through this, too.

One night, I fell asleep while praying. Then I just shot up in bed. I looked at the clock. It was three in the morning.

I woke up and said to myself, *I'm going back to school.* Just like that. I was talking to myself. But the message was clear, and it somehow felt like my salvation.

Once I knew I was going back to school, the decision was where to go. I had connections at the Interdenominational Theological Center (ITC) at the Atlanta University Center. Morehouse School of Religion was one of the five seminaries at ITC. I knew I could get in without any issues. I told Reverend Brown, an associate minister at Tabernacle, who had graduated from there and was very popular, that I planned to enroll. I asked him to take me to the admissions office. I filled out the application, and it was accepted. I started school that fall.

When I hit that campus, people knew who I was because what had happened with Dennis was all over town, all over the faith community. Anyone who was in clergy would have known about what I was dealing with. I was in the middle of the divorce at that time, as well.

I had someone take over the day-to-day work at my child-care business, which was thriving, while I took five classes—a full load, like I didn't have anything else to do.

Again, work was my drug of choice. I started going to school at night while still working part-time during the day. I enjoyed it immensely. Missiology, philosophy, the New Testament. We had a course in using the library, and a course where we explored our calling and what we were trying to do. I can't remember the name of that class, but I took it. We had to take Ministry and Context, which put a practical purpose to our decision to come to seminary.

In my first philosophy class, the professor talked about how he'd found out his wife was a lesbian. He explained how initially it had a negative impact because it affected the way he was treating his female students. I don't know what caused him to share this story that first day in class. He said a lot of things that touched me.

"I healed because God loved me more than I loved myself," he told us.

That made me cry. How is that possible? His words helped me get through what I was going through. They helped me to sleep. They helped me to keep moving every day. Each day got a little bit easier. Every day it was a little better.

I finished the three-year program in two years.

When I got on campus, I knew I was supposed to be there. I felt a release. It was a healing place because of the content, and I felt supported there. The campus was nice and calm and inviting. I just felt safe there.

The professors I had were phenomenal. These men and women had studied at Emory University, Harvard University, and Vanderbilt University. I got a good theological education. The things I learned about the New and Old Testaments, and the history of the Bible, how it was canonized, and the history of religion and the Christian faith, were invaluable.

I learned that the words were indeed inspired by God, but that the writers brought their biases to the text. You must read the Bible with that in mind, understanding those biases and getting to the heart of what God is really saying.

It's a serious enterprise to interpret the Bible and not mislead God's people. The central message of the text is a message of justice. A message of love. A message of God loving God's people and wanting to be reconciled with God's people. I was also taught to not speak of God in masculine terms. God is beyond gender. God is bigger than race or gender or sexuality or any mortal definition.

Seminary was an enlightening experience.

It freed me of certain notions about women that had been perpetuated for so long. People have used the Bible for so long to promote their hatred. If you hate women, you can go through the Bible and find/lift a whole bunch of scriptures that appear to support your belief that God hates women too. We fought against those notions in seminary.

If you believe that God hates gays, you can definitely find scripture that appears to support that, too. And that is what is being taught from pulpit to pulpit throughout the world: that God hates gays and homosexuality is a sin.

I was on a mission to change the theological interpretation that homosexuality is a sin. I wanted to break that kind of thinking. I knew it could be done, because through my reading and experience, I had a change of heart myself. I wanted an education so I could dissect the Bible and find out where these thoughts were coming from and how to stop oppressive communications. I had to start from the beginning.

I do not believe that homosexuality is a sin, any more than I believe that being a woman in the pulpit is a sin; any more than I believe that having a glass of wine is a sin; and any more than I believe that committing suicide is a sin and that anyone that commits suicide is doomed forever. No one kills himself or herself unless he or she is mentally or emotionally disturbed or sick. It's an illness. If you don't condemn someone for having heart disease, then how can you condemn someone for having mind disease?

I wanted to get us back to the basics of God's word, the foundation, which is love.

"God so loved the world . . ." If you're going to lift any text, lift that one. It's a "whosoever" kind of text. Inclusive. There's nothing discriminating about that.

When you hurt someone by being mean and vicious, I think that is the real sin.

If I fail to do what God has called me to do, to serve God's people, I have committed a sin against God and myself. I'm human. I will make mistakes; when I get mad, I will curse. But I don't believe God is going to send me to hell for that. I think what will land me in hell is not loving people.

When I graduated, I had the highest GPA in my class, and my master's thesis paper—"A Model of Christian Education: How to Help the Black Church Love and Accept the LGBT (Lesbian, Gay, Bisexual, and Transgender) Population"—won a school award.

How many feel estranged from God because they believe what church and society teaches about their race, their color, their gender, their sexuality—physical characteristics determined at birth? Does that make sense?

That was why I was so pleased to be involved in the Love and Acceptance Ministry at Tabernacle. At this time, Tabernacle was the only openly gay black church in the area with the only openly gay pastor. Dennis had come out by this point. I wasn't there for the announcement, but I know he did it from the pulpit and it must have been moving for people, because the church was flourishing.

He invited me to join him as copastor in this Love and Acceptance Ministry.

I truly believed that God had founded Tabernacle through the God-called agencies of Lydia Meredith and Dennis Meredith—through both of our blood, sweat, and many tears. I came to know that this was God's plan for joining my life with Dennis's—not our marriage, but our ministry.

It was a chance to promote the liberation and justice I had just studied. It was time to tackle the last frontier of bigotry that needed to be infiltrated, dismantled, and broken down.

People still look at me in awe when they see me visit Tabernacle and lend support to my sons who work there and my grandchildren who are now also an integral part of the church. They look at me in awe that I was able to come back and support my ex-husband and his partner.

And I guess it is pretty amazing to see, knowing the history.

I see the transgender population sleeping in front of our door on the weekends at my downtown childcare facility. They are homeless and cannot go into the shelter. They are not safe there. But there is a place they can go for shelter, for love, and for acceptance. That place is Tabernacle. Tabernacle welcomes them and loves them.

I'm not saying it's right to be promiscuous. Or that it's okay to have multiple affairs. You're not doing unto others as you would have others do unto you. Whether you're gay, straight, black, white, or indifferent, if you're hurting yourself and you're hurting somebody else, that's not right. You don't have the right to do that.

But we need to understand that a lot of people are hurting. They are turned into Frankensteins when they're not loved. They are turned into monsters. We create the monsters in the world. We create the mass murderers. We create them. Society, with its corruption, hypocrisy, and hatred, creates the monsters.

It's almost like what Malcolm X said about the chickens coming home to roost when President John F. Kennedy was assassinated. We put it out there and are surprised when it comes back. We create communities where people are treated in inhumane ways. What you're sowing, you get back. You sow hate, that's what you get back. If you sow dysfunction, that's what you get back.

If you don't give a child what he or she needs, guess what? That child may just grow up to be very damaged and then go on to damage others. It's a cycle.

It doesn't feel good to know that I have sons who are promiscuous. But, Daddy was promiscuous. It didn't happen in a vacuum. They were taught that behavior through actions, by observation. Children are not stupid. They watch, listen, and learn everything you do in that home—whether you know it or not.

Dennis had the nerve to tell our eldest son to marry his girlfriend, whom he consistently cheats on, suggesting that monogamy is unrealistic. My son told Dennis, "Dad, I love her. But if I marry her, I may cheat on her."

He didn't think he could be faithful.

He felt predisposed to follow what his daddy did. And Dennis followed what his daddy did. And I'm sure Dennis's daddy's daddy was the same kind of man.

Generation after generation of men are socialized to abuse their wives and/or girlfriends. They are socialized to believe they can treat women any way they want to. The cycle needs to be broken, because I don't want my grandsons to follow suit.

I pray about it every night.

I live in truth. So when my eldest son had one of his girlfriends come over, I told her that he had a serious girlfriend and that they had children together. My son didn't speak to me for a while after that because the girl called and told him it was over. She told him she felt like a slut and a home-wrecker. I thought she should know. My children know I will not keep their secrets. I keep no secrets. Not anymore.

I told Dennis exactly what I told that girl. And he said, "You told her right." He knew what was right, but he didn't tell his son that. There's a difference between what people profess and what people do. Dennis knew what was right to tell our son. But he told him and advised him to be an infidel.

That's why I had to go back to school and pursue the full truth and get understanding.

A lot of people who are not in church don't go because of the kind of hypocrisy I'm talking about. And I can't blame them. When I see people who don't go to church, I understand. I've lived it. I've lived with these ministers with no moral development, living these double and triple lives as they stand in the pulpit on Sundays preaching quite a different message.

Morality is also a developmental domain. Most of these ministers have zero moral development. And the community does not hold them accountable. Dennis had a church full of folks. But they didn't tithe. They said they loved him. But they wouldn't give.

When I went back to Tabernacle for that short period to support the Love and Acceptance Ministry as the copastor, the offerings tripled. The same amount of people, but they started to give. I wasn't preaching about tithing. I was preaching truth. I was feeding the flock. I wasn't telling them what they wanted to hear. I was giving them what they needed—truth!

After Dennis's final betrayal (yes, just when I thought he could sink no lower, he did—it's still too painful to talk about), I had to find a new church home. I could no longer stand in that pulpit at Tabernacle and support hypocrisy. I only came back on a promise. Again, another promise broken.

But I found another church. There are other churches preaching the truth. I attend one now, the Buckhead Church in Atlanta. Andy Stanley is the pastor there.

The pastor is held accountable to live morally by the church. Proverbs says there is safety in counsel. You have to be open to counsel. The text also warns against the counsel of the wicked. But if you're in appropriate counsel, it will make you a better person.

CHAPTER SIXTEEN

To Forgive . . .

After I graduated from seminary at the top of my class in 2009, my life was finally getting back on track. I had started dating a pastor and was attending his church. Just as I was on my way to happy, here comes Dennis.

He had this grand plan of starting a ministry with me where we trained other pastors to deliver this message of love and acceptance that we would spread in the United States, and then we would take the message global. He believed the world—particularly the Christian world—needed to be "informed" and heal around this issue of sexuality.

Initially I told him no. I didn't want to get sucked back into his web. But the more he talked about his plan, the more excited I got about the possibilities. This was what I'd gone to school to do. And I was uniquely trained to help launch this movement. It had become a passion of mine, and Dennis was speaking to it. He talked of the entire family coming together to create this movement. Each of my sons had a role to help pull it all together.

Part of this, I believe now, was Dennis's plot to end my relationship with the pastor I had been seeing. He had been telling me that he thought this man was no-good. He had a lot of nerve, huh?

The other part was to bring me back to save Tabernacle. Since I'd left, not only had the congregation dwindled, but the members who had stayed had stopped tithing. The church was in a financial crisis, and bringing me back, Dennis hoped, would revitalize Tabernacle.

I love Tabernacle and I love my family. I had been away from my church family since filing for divorce. I couldn't stand to be there among the stares and whispers. Dennis, who was now living openly as a gay man, had his lover still prominently in the church. What would I look like sitting in a pew every Sunday? I just couldn't do it.

I couldn't see a way to ever go back, until Dennis came to me with this new ministry movement. I knew the church missed me. I was in so many ways the church mother. It would be a win-win situation for Dennis if I decided to actually do it. He had hired a publicist who would pull it all together for us and promote it. We would be ready to go in a few months, he said.

The Sunday after we had our big meeting about me coming back, Dennis announced to the church during a shocking sermon that he had made a big mistake. He said that he had ended his relationship with Lamont and that the church would now be his primary focus and his only partner. He also announced that I would return to serve as copastor. Now, we had just *discussed* this. I had initially said no, and I'd agreed that I would *think* about it. I hadn't agreed to actually come back. I'd told Dennis I had to talk to the man I was seeing first and that I would pray about it and let him know.

The response to his announcement was overwhelming. My sons, who were working still at Tabernacle, ran home and told me how excited and energized the entire congregation was over this announcement.

Once again, I allowed Dennis to manipulate me into doing something. I would have probably consented, but I had wanted to take my time and really think it through. But after his grand announcement I felt as if I had no choice. Within the first month of me coming back, the congregation grew and was happy. Offerings tripled. The man I was seeing broke up with me. He warned me that Dennis was only manipulating me for his own gain and that he didn't want to be around to watch. That broke my heart.

But I threw myself into the ministry—calling on colleagues from the seminary to train the leadership for this new mission. Within that first month, we had nearly a hundred leaders to train and ordain. All of this was to culminate in a big event to celebrate the launch of a global Love and Acceptance Ministry.

The eve before the big event where everything would come together, I discovered perhaps the biggest betrayal yet. I discovered that Dennis was still in a relationship with Lamont. It had all been a lie. I was livid. I wasn't mad because I hoped that we would reconcile (even though Dennis often talked about it). After he left in 2005, I never looked back. Thanks to therapy! I was completely over him. But I think he was having a hard time not having his cake and eating it too. He was having a hard time not being able to always fall back into my arms whenever he wanted.

I was livid because after all we had been through, the one thing I hoped for was that we could be friends—friends enough to not lie to one another. Here he was, lying again. Here he was, making it impossible now for me to even work to build this ministry with him—something that was so important to me.

Once again, I was left with nowhere to go. I had to leave Tabernacle . . . again. The man I'd been seeing was the pastor of the church I had been attending before going back to Tabernacle. So I couldn't go back there. My family was once again torn to shreds. My oldest son, Taylor, cursed out and almost struck his father for ruining his life. He, too, had committed his whole future to this new ministry concept. And now it was destroyed. Taylor was also now without a church home, because he couldn't go back.

Taylor and I decided to visit the Buckhead Church, pastored by Andy Stanley, the son of Dr. Charles Stanley. Andy Stanley was young, smart, and a progressive thinker. He was refreshing. I could not attend any church that bashed gay folk, and I found that the Buckhead Church (which is part of the North Point Ministries, the second-largest church in America) didn't preach against homosexuals.

A few Sundays in, Andy preached about his mission.

"My goal is not to become the largest church, but the most benevolent church," he said.

That's the Sunday I decided to join. I went through new-members class. In that class along with me was a gay white man who had just lost his lover to AIDS and was threatening suicide. He would openly swear at all of our sessions. Yet the leaders didn't even flinch, nor were they disturbed by his outbursts of rage and anger. There was a lesbian couple, a Latino man who'd been raised a Catholic, a woman who had been just released from jail for physically abusing her child. There was a married couple where the husband was saved and the wife was agnostic, and there was a young couple who were living together and unmarried—she was a tennis pro and a volunteer at my school.

While Dennis was trying to put together his Love and Acceptance Ministry globally, I was witnessing a living and breathing one—with no fanfare. No public relations reps. The ministry was all about loving people and accepting them.

Needless to say, my new-member's class was the bomb. I enjoyed the dialogue and sharing my theological thoughts with this group—especially having just finished seminary. The experience was stimulating and it was just what I needed to get over losing my boyfriend, losing my church, and losing my way. In my heart, I knew this was where God intended for me to be, to heal.

During my first few months as a new member, Andy had preached a number of series (he loved to preach series). Like with a soap opera, you'd come back to hear and see what was going to happen the next week. This series was called "Future Families." He described this new world where the notion of what a family looked like had dramatically changed.

"There isn't the traditional, mom, dad, and kids anymore," he said. Andy told the story of close friends of his, where the husband decided to leave his family to marry another man. He shared how the wife was bitter at first. But she attended a support group for divorced women. There she met another woman who had just gotten a divorce. This woman spent the entire session complaining about and cursing her ex-husband. Each session this woman nursed her wounds, reliving the painful events over and over and over.

After about a year, the woman from Andy's church, who had met a new man and had gotten remarried, asked Pastor Andy to invite her ex-husband and his partner to church, and she came with her new husband and their children. This became the beginning to bridging the great divide within their family. That Sunday, the family worshipped together. Soon they would share a meal together after church. Then they were sharing holidays together. Before they knew it, the whole definition of that family changed.

Andy asked the wife what had made her decide to invite her ex-husband to church. She said, "I saw that woman in the support group, week after week reliving her pain, angry, bitter, hostile, and I just decided that I didn't want to be like her."

I listened to that story and I sat there thinking about how my family had been ripped to shreds. How I had tried to hold it together, but how my anger and bitterness over what my husband had done to me, to our marriage, and to our lives, had left a gaping hole in what used to be a tight-knit unit. A family.

I had to make a decision. Did I want to hold on to my pride, my pain, my perception of what I wanted? Or was I going to deal with my new reality and bring my family back together?

This particular sermon was a six-part lesson on reconciliation. I got the CD of it and I listened to it over and over and over again. My pastor talked about how we use all kinds of excuses for why we don't reconcile with the people who hurt us.

We say, "I don't want you to think I condone what you did." So we detach ourselves from them. I was doing that. I felt that if I forgave Dennis and even Lamont, for whom I still held much bitterness and disgust, I would somehow be letting Dennis know that what he'd done was okay.

What they were doing was *not* okay. But, as my pastor said, you can forgive someone and reconcile with them and still not condone their behavior. These two things are not connected.

What really got me was learning that being unforgiving is wicked. The parable of the unforgiving servant who begged his master to forgive his debts but refused to forgive a debt owed to him in Matthew 18:21–35 was a great example of this. In the end, when the master found out that the servant hadn't forgiven the debt of one of his debtors, he handed that unforgiving servant over to jailers to be tortured. And then Jesus said: "This is how my heavenly Father will treat each of you unless you forgive your brother or sister from your heart."

This teaching convinced me to try to forgive. What Dennis and Lamont had done was wicked. But what I was doing was equally wicked. When Peter asked Him, "Lord, how many times shall I forgive my brother or sister who sins against me? Up to seven times?" Jesus answered, "I tell you, not seven times, but seventy-seven times."

I needed to forgive. We all must forgive. Pastor Andy reminded me of this, saying, "Because God reconciled with us while we were still sinners, Jesus paid the debt we were not fit to pay."

Because of Jesus's redemptive act of love (giving His life), humankind *can* be reconciled to God—even in our imperfect state. No matter what you do, you can be reconciled with God. I decided to put this into action.

The holidays were coming around, and this was a particularly tough time for me. When Dennis and I were still together, our holidays were some of the most memorable times ever. We always did Thanksgiving and Christmas in a big way with the boys.

I remember one Thanksgiving, Dennis booked airline tickets for the family to spend time in New York City for the Macy's Thanksgiving Day Parade extravaganza. I fought the idea with everything in me. I thought it was over the top, but we had the best time of our lives.

Christmas was my time to show my love for my family. I would plan the dinner and events of the holiday like the sacred event that it was. Christmas was the Meredith family's favorite holiday. One Christmas, when the boys were old enough to buy gifts, we were not allowed to spend more than $10 for any gift, because Dennis wanted to teach the boys that the holiday was not all about the presents. Instead, we spent time over dinner telling each other what we loved most about one another. Before we even got to the actual meal there would be so much emotion and so many tears. We had to work hard to compose ourselves for the feast that followed. The whole holiday was family-centered.

My pastor, as part of this series on forgiveness, gave us homework. He suggested that we start reconciling by inviting those from whom we were estranged for holiday dinner. Andy would always give homework assignments in his sermons, something we would have to practice, something we would have to remember, something we would have to do to bring the message of the sermon home.

"And don't worry about whether or not they come," he said. "It doesn't matter if they respond. The act of inviting them is what frees you. The act of reconciling works in you. Your spiritual place changes by doing it."

I sent a text message to the whole family, including Dennis: "I'm hosting Christmas dinner and everybody and their partners are invited."

It was a simple message. But it was also a clear message.

Micah responded first.

"Yeah! Mama is cooking!"

He was so excited. My other sons confirmed that they would be there. I knew that wouldn't be a problem. None of them ever missed a chance to eat my cooking. A week passed and I hadn't gotten a response from Dennis. Two weeks passed and finally I got a simple text from Dennis that read: "We're coming."

The boys started buzzing around. They were excited and

couldn't believe it was happening. They also let me in on what was happening with their father. They told me that Lamont had told Dennis that he did not want to come. Dennis was really hurt that Lamont would not consent to come, and he'd spent the last two weeks trying to convince him to change his mind.

To me it was another admission of wrongdoing. Lamont must have had shame and guilt to the point that he couldn't face me. Knowing that he had some remorse helped me to feel better about my decision to invite him to dinner.

I started pulling together my recipes. I was going to do the core meal, but I sent out an e-mail telling everyone what I wanted them to bring.

I asked Dennis to bring chitterlings and coleslaw. The boys loved chitterlings (especially their father's). I've never had the stomach to clean or cook them. Despite Lamont saying he wasn't coming, I still asked him to bring wine and ice.

A couple of days before Christmas, the boys told me that Lamont definitely was not coming. They said that Dennis was having Christmas breakfast at his house and had asked them to invite me.

"If you go to Dad's house, maybe Lamont would feel okay about coming to dinner at ours," Micah said.

"I'm cooking—I'm going to be so tired," I said. "I don't know . . ."

I could tell they wanted me to go. So I said okay.

Christmas Eve, I got a text from Lamont saying he was

coming, and he thanked me for the invitation. "I will be honored to come," he said.

Christmas Day, I went with my sons to the house Dennis shared with Lamont. This was to be an icebreaker, and I was nervous and unsure about going. It was hard for me to go there. But I knew my boys needed that. It went okay. I did notice, however, that Lamont couldn't make eye contact with me. Dennis was his usual gregarious self and kept the conversation going, but Lamont and I didn't connect at all.

I left early to finish my cooking and take a nap.

Thirty minutes before folks were scheduled to arrive for dinner at my house, Dennis called. I think he had me on speakerphone as he told me that his "family" (meaning Lamont) was giving him a hard time about coming.

"I understand, if you're not able to come," I said. "But we would really be disappointed if you and your family did not come."

They showed up and brought the chitterlings, the coleslaw, the wine and ice, and gifts for everyone under the Christmas tree.

Dinner ended up being beautiful. There was not this big elephant in the room that we had to manage. We'd started killing that elephant at breakfast. We ate, we laughed, and we shared gifts after dinner. It was a good feeling.

When everyone left and I was alone, I felt this huge weight lift from my spirit. I'd survived it. I had finally gotten free.

Mercy and Truth

Let not mercy and truth forsake thee: bind them
about thy neck; write them upon the table of thine heart:
So shalt thou find favour and good understanding
in the sight of God and man.

—Proverbs 3:3-4

Reverend Butler would travel from Alabama to attend classes at the seminary during the week and commute back to lead his church on the weekend. He drove a fine new white Cadillac. He would show up for class dressed to kill—in the finest tailored suits. He walked into that classroom with his chest puffed out and his head held high. He was the rock star of our class and no one could tell him different.

Reverend Butler would testify in class about the great work Jesus had done in his life, blessing him with riches and even delivering him from being physically abusive to his wife. I watched him hit on and flirt with the handful of women in the class—despite having a wife and children back in Alabama. There was even a rumor that he'd gotten a fellow seminarian pregnant. The woman ended up getting an abortion, so there was no baby to answer for.

I was already turned off by his pompous attitude, but his false piety and hypocrisy made me sick to my stomach. I vowed that one day I would run my own seminary to screen candidates whose only agenda was the three Ps—"Possessions, Power, and Pussy." And for those who happened to "slip in" and find themselves in a seminary seat, I would add curricula to convict their spirit and teach them the true meaning of a call to ministry.

I hated group assignments because many of my classmates were slackers and I ended up doing most of the work. And Reverend Butler was the worst of them all. Heaven forbid we have an exam and the professor leave the room. The professor thought that was safe because it was, after all, a room full of preachers and preachers-to-be. They would never think of cheating, right? Think again. No sooner did our professor leave the room, on our final exam, than the Reverend Butler was leaning over whispering to classmates for the answers. He wasn't the only one. In fact, it was not unusual for my classmates to cheat and make up lies for why assignments were missed. You might expect this behavior from regular students, but certainly not from people who claimed to love God and who wanted to lead a church. These people's aim was not good leadership, education, and training that would prepare for excellence in leadership, but the three Ps.

During my time in seminary, I knew there was a real problem in the church. I got to see it up close. People were there for all the wrong reasons. I went back to seminary to get some answers to some tough questions being debated in the religious community and in my own life. But all I was coming up with were more questions. The biggest question I had was: Why were so many people going into ministry who had absolutely no desire to help people?

The notion of helping people was not even a consideration. Some male classmates believed they existed to be served, and not vice versa, to give service. Some women there seemed to be interested in, simply, finding a husband.

On many occasions, I would see female classmates excessively primping in the lounge instead of preparing for course work. Discussions outside of the classroom among these women had nothing to do with the lecture or lesson. But there was a whole lot of talk about the lecturer and how good he looked, or wondering if he was single. Most seminary professors not only taught but also served as pastors in churches throughout the city. Some were talented, handsome, and eligible and for some of these women, that was reason enough to show up. They had no interest in being pastors. They simply wanted to marry one.

After completing my seminary degree, I continued my studies in public policy/nonprofit management. I wanted to sustain my school and strengthen my leadership of nonprofit organizations. I also wanted to network with the philanthropic community.

I came across this interesting fact in one of my classes: Out of more than 800,000 religious nonprofits, less than 5 percent were involved in building/improving communities. Less than 5 percent! The other 95 percent just existed with no purpose beyond the church walls.

There's something seriously wrong when the very institutions that are supposed to be there to build and transform communities and serve people in distress are so far removed from that mission. How many pastors are driving Rolls-Royces and Bentleys while their congregations are mired in poverty? How many pastors are living in mansions while their congregations are barely making ends meet? And let's expand beyond the congregation.

How many churches are on blocks where there are liquor stores and drug hangouts on the corner? How is it possible to have so much poverty and blight and despair where there's a church? Staggering are the statistics in this nation about juvenile delinquency, unwed-teen births, blighted neighborhoods with crack houses (half burned down and half with boarded-up windows and doors), children and their families living in poverty, unemployment, truancy, high rates of dropouts from middle and high school, and the list goes on, and on, and on. Because more pastors are concerned with power, possessions, and pussy than they are with helping people.

When I was coming up, it wasn't unusual for the church to get involved with politics and social issues. The civil rights movement grew through churches throughout the south. The church was the epicenter of power in the black community. It was where people went to get direction—not just spiritual direction.

My little church in Macon had a commitment to the community. Even my womanizing pastor had training programs for men in the community, owned real estate, and provided affordable, safe, and clean housing for the community. There was a commitment to family and community.

Adam Clayton Powell Jr. was pastor of one of Harlem's largest churches, Abyssinian Baptist Church, in the 1950s. He took over after his father retired. Powell enlarged his father's ministry with his food and clothing initiatives for the poor and working class in his community.

He led rent strikes against slumlords in Harlem. He led boycotts and picketed businesses that excluded blacks and was the chairman of the Coordinating Committee for Employment, organizing to put pressure on major corporations and businesses to employ blacks in positions above domestic and menial labor. Powell led a bus boycott in Harlem, which led to the New York City Transit Authority hiring more than two hundred blacks. He even put pressure on local drugstores to hire black pharmacists.

Adam Clayton Powell Jr. was a pastor, a preacher, who worked for his community. I'm sure he loved the power, and we know about his weakness for women, but he didn't forsake his congregation or community. He worked *for* the people. He wasn't perfect, but I believe he was a prime example of the impact a pastor can have when he or she puts God, the church and its community, and people first. Powell did even more once he got to the United States Congress, working on everything from Head Start to Medicaid and establishing a minimum wage. But it started with him in the pulpit.

Perhaps the greatest modern example of what a pastor can accomplish when he or she sets a community agenda is the work of Dr. Martin Luther King Jr. He also followed in his father's footsteps, becoming a pastor. He took over Dexter Avenue Baptist Church in Montgomery, Alabama, at the age of twenty-five, and was thrust into the growing civil rights movement, becoming its face and its soul, using the teachings of Jesus Christ as the backdrop to the nonviolence movement.

His unwavering commitment to community and justice

moved a nation toward freedom and opportunity. Many black clergy who saw his efforts as "troublemaking" and "rabble-rousing" heavily criticized his involvement at the time. Dr. King's work extended to all aspects of equality. He wasn't satisfied with blacks being able to sit at a lunch counter or wherever they wanted on a bus. He asked this question: "What good is having the right to sit at a lunch counter if you can't afford to buy a hamburger?" And he led a poor people's movement that started in his community but expanded to all the poor within the greater community—the entire nation.

Keep in mind that King was doing all of this in his twenties and thirties. He was a young man, committed to improving the conditions of his community.

Beyond what the church and pastors of today are *not* doing, what they're actually doing is destroying the church. The debauchery, the greed, the adultery, infidelity, the idolatry are rampant. The lack of morality within the church is unbelievable. I know one distinguished pastor in Atlanta who is on his third divorce. If you speak to him, he will tell you that not one of his failed marriages was his fault. Before his third divorce was final, he had the audacity to approach me for sex, saying "I love pussy." So I'm not speaking based on rumor. I'm all for no judgment, but we are called to be accountable and responsible as faith citizens.

The church has also become the seat of oppression instead of the home of justice and liberation (racism, anti-Semitism, sexism, heterosexism, and just about every "ism" imaginable are practiced and oftentimes "defended" by the church). Famed writer Anne Rice said this about her faith: "I quit Christianity because it is anti-gay, anti-Semitic, and anti-feminist." I get what she's saying. I sometimes feel embarrassed to call myself a Christian. So Pastor Andy Stanley suggested calling ourselves simply Jesus followers.

The faith community must stop covering up, hiding, and ignoring the gross indiscretions within the faith community, because it is literally ripping the church apart. Proverbs 3:3–4 says tell the truth. Unveil it. According to Pastor Andy Stanley, we should have mercy (shutting out hatred and selfishness); but also, we should live and tell the truth (shutting out deception and hypocrisy).

There is tension between mercy and truth. So be it. It keeps both ideals functioning. Pastors would argue the "don't judge" notion here. Not judging does not mean you ignore reckless behavior.

When Jesus came across the woman who was about to be stoned for adultery in the Book of John, chapter eight, what did he say to her after all of her accusers left in shame? Jesus said, "Neither do I condemn you. Go your way, and from now on do not sin again." He didn't judge her: "Neither do I condemn you." But neither did Jesus let her off the hook. He told her to "sin" no more.

What happened to the "sin no more" part? Some churches

have become a place of mercy, but not a place of truth and accountability. Some churches have truth and accountability, but no mercy. Some churches have neither.

Pastor Andy Stanley says, "Truth and mercy are like two sides of a coin." They must coexist to function as God intended: so that humankind will favor the community of God. Another biblical version says it this way, paraphrased, when you practice mercy and truth, "Then you will win favor and a good name in the sight of God and humankind."

The truth is that as a pastor/leader/layperson, you should not be a predator, but be a faithful faith citizen, setting an example for ethical and moral living. That's the truth. Mercy is that we all fall short, we sin and make mistakes—and we will be forgiven. Without the practice of mercy and truth, the church community will continue to lose favor with God and with humankind.

Eight Signs That Your Partner May Be Gay

I spent a lot of time during my marriage being clueless. Some of it was willful cluelessness, where I really didn't want to confront the obvious. I didn't want to admit what was actually going on in my relationship.

But some of the cluelessness came from really not knowing. As a woman from a certain generation, there were just things that I never thought I'd have to confront. But having lived this life and this lie, I would now like to share just a few signs that would have been helpful for me to pay attention to when I was married to a man who I later found out was gay/bisexual.

1. Long/extended absences and trips

Whether there is a rational excuse or not—"I'm going on this trip for my job"—a spouse should always be wary of multiple and extended trips, whether they are overnight, on the weekends, or for weeks at a time. A person who really loves his or her home won't so quickly leave it. That should be something you should investigate in your relationship if it happens frequently.

Dennis would go out of town (even to other countries) at least four times a year and hook up with other pastors who were gay. They told their wives they were on spiritual retreats. But I later found out these trips were masquerades for full weeks of gay sexual escapades.

At the time, I was comforted that Dennis was traveling with other pastors. I thought it was great he was networking. I was always looking for him to further this career. But what he was really doing was exploring his sexuality.

2. A change in sexual appetite

If your spouse suddenly stops wanting to have sex with you or all of a sudden is on sexual overdrive, you should raise an eyebrow and pay attention.

With Dennis, the more he was out there, the more he seemed to want to have sex with me. Early in our relationship he had a voracious sexual appetite. I discovered that at the point where he was being the most promiscuous with men, he was the most sexually active with me. Perhaps he was trying to prove something to himself, or perhaps he was covering up for what he was doing.

When he fell in love with Lamont, the exact opposite happened. He didn't seem to ever want to have sex with me. And when he tried, he couldn't function. I chalked it up to age. But there was definitely something more going on. He was coming to grips with really being gay, and once he confronted that truth, it was harder and harder for him to pretend.

As in a heterosexual affair, the wife of a closeted gay man becomes abused and neglected when her mate falls in love with someone else. For me, it didn't matter that the other woman was a man.

3. A history of molestation

Dennis confessed in one of our counseling sessions that he'd been molested by two family members at different times growing up. And the sexual abuse had lasted until he was fifteen years old.

Sexual exploitation leaves scars, especially when untreated.

Our son Micah disclosed that he'd been exploited by a teenage boy in our church when he was little. I encouraged him to get therapy at the time he told me, but he refused. Now that he is seeking a stable relationship, he is in counseling.

I don't believe in Micah's case that the molestation led to him being gay. As I mentioned, he was effeminate from birth and never seemed sexually interested in girls—even though that's all he hung out with as a kid. But what the molestation did do was sexualize my child at an early age. Micah confessed that he liked it. And it probably confused him. Perhaps Micah would have been more selective about his sexual partners if that hadn't happened to him. Perhaps he would not have contracted HIV. I wonder about that.

But Dennis's story is not unique. I find that so many closeted gay men were sexually abused. There is no guarantee that a boy or girl who is abused will become gay, but if they don't deal with the molestation, they will more likely than not become dysfunctional partners, prone to bringing that unresolved baggage into relationships with them. Straight or gay, that's not a good formula for success.

4. He is angry and almost hostile in his condemnation of same-sex lifestyles

Dennis would often talk about the promiscuity of his uncles and friends, while he was guilty of the same behavior and worse.

I guess talking about their indiscretions made him feel better about his own. He would also tell me about gay pastors whose wives were covers. He would tell me with disgust, all the while he was doing the exact same thing.

When he noticed that Micah was effeminate growing up, he would constantly stay on him to "man up." He really rode Micah about acting "like a girl."

Dennis preached a sermon once titled, "I Live in a Haunted House." He said that the Holy Ghost would not allow entrance of certain visitors into your house (your body), like homosexuality. The haunted house was a metaphor for himself—needless to say, the Holy "Ghost" was not the ghost that haunted Dennis's house.

Once, while visiting my in-laws in Toledo, I called Dennis a "cream puff"—a term I'd heard my father use to describe a person with a loud bark and no bite. Dennis's father got so angry with me for calling his son that. To Big June, a cream puff was a homosexual. He didn't want his son called that.

And Dennis wasn't having it either. I hadn't meant it in that way. But he, and apparently his father, was sensitive to how he was perceived. Dennis was constantly saying negative things about people who seemed outwardly gay, which is probably why he worked so hard on his physique and appearance, to not seem gay to the outside world.

5. He watches and reads porn. A lot.

You have to watch what your spouse reads and watches and how he/she entertains himself/herself. I used to believe that men just were perverse and that it was okay for them to watch porn and do things like visit massage parlors—because men are wired differently.

But those videos, books, magazines, websites, and other outlets are simply gateways. Pay close attention if your man is into all of that. Watch exactly what he's watching. Watch it with him and see for yourself.

When I found those gay movies that Dennis was hiding in the garage, that was more than a sign. There are many more ways for a man to hide his tendencies today. But if you want to know who you're living with, you have to be a bit of a detective and pay attention. Don't wait until you're beaten over the head with it, the way I was. I know a woman who discovered that her husband had been visiting gay websites on his computer. That forced him to tell her the truth.

That's all we want. You just want to know what you're dealing with so that you can decide for yourself.

6. Associations

Pay close attention to the friends, visitors, and acquaintances your spouse attempts to bring into the family circle.

I discovered that Dennis found it easier for himself if he

brought his lovers around under the guise of a friend or associate. It was a lot easier for me to not pay attention if that friend also happened to be a pastor. I never gave it a second thought. But Dennis would invite these people over to the house so that I would get to know them and then be comfortable if he hung out with them or they went on a trip or a conference together.

Many musicians whom Dennis slept with stayed at our home. He would hire them to play for the church. Every gay man Dennis slept with called my house or was in my face at some point in their relationship.

I hear this is a very popular tactic—for men, in particular, living a double life. Watch their "best friend," particularly a new best friend.

7. *Pay attention to your spouse's body*

If you find your spouse is turning up with unexplained rashes or diseases, such as crabs, alarms should be going off for you. As you know, Dennis gave me sexually transmitted diseases. Each time, he had an excuse that seemed to make sense. For the crabs, the explanation of how he contracted the disease was that he got it from sitting on a toilet seat. All I had to do was some research to find out that this explanation was completely unscientific and ridiculous. But I trusted my husband and I believed him.

But when I had to be treated for gonorrhea, I should have gotten out of there.

Before you contract something from your spouse, pay close attention to his body and see if there are any changes. Unfortunately, some diseases cannot be easily detected. You may not know until you have symptoms or he tells you.

With the kinds of sexually transmitted diseases out here, it's too risky not to pay attention. I consider myself lucky. Because Dennis could well have given me something from which I could still be suffering today.

It's not just diseases you should pay attention to. One pastor friend told me that his wife, who he later found out was gay, would take off for the weekends and return home with her body bruised and scratched up from rough sex. A lot of times the person your spouse is cheating with wants to leave their mark. That goes for straight couples as well.

8. Mood swings

Sometimes Dennis seemed very happy, but other times he seemed very sad. He recently explained why: "Living a double life was not easy." He told me for most of his life he contemplated suicide; and that while battling cancer, he promised God, "God if you let me live, I promise I will be a voice for gay men and women in America." Today, Dennis only thinks about living.